HANDEL

THE CONCERTGOER'S COMPANIONS
SERIES EDITOR ALEC HYATT KING

BEETHOVEN by Rosemary Hughes

BRAHMS by Kathleen Dale

HANDEL by Charles Cudworth

HAYDN by Brian Redfern

MOZART by Alec Hyatt King

BACH by Alec Robertson and Robert Anderson

HANDEL

A biography, with a survey of
books, editions and recordings

by

CHARLES CUDWORTH

CLIVE BINGLEY  LONDON

FIRST PUBLISHED 1972 BY CLIVE BINGLEY LTD

16 PEMBRIDGE ROAD LONDON W11

SET IN 10 ON 13 POINT LINOTYPE TIMES

AND PRINTED IN THE UK BY

THE CENTRAL PRESS (ABERDEEN) LTD

COPYRIGHT © CHARLES CUDWORTH 1972

ALL RIGHTS RESERVED

0 85157 137 9

CONTENTS

Handel's life   *page* 7

Books in English about Handel   *page* 44

Editions of Handel's music   *page* 57

Selected recordings of Handel's music   *page* 90

Index   *page* 103

To my dear wife who has put up
with me (and Mr Handel) for more
years than she will care to remember . . .

Handel's Life

Halle-in-Saxony (or Halle 'an-die-Saale', Halle on the river
Saale—as it is often called, to distinguish it from another Halle, in
Westphalia) was a reasonably prosperous place in the late seventeenth century, and was just beginning to recover from the ravages
of the Thirty Years War, which had left Germany so much behind
economically compared to the rest of Europe. Situated not far from
Leipzig, Halle derived prosperity and importance from its salt-
springs, which had long been used in the manufacture of salt, an
all-important commodity in medieval and renaissance economy.
It had already become a fine city by the time of Handel's birth, and
boasted a handsome medieval town hall, as well as a number of
imposing churches, chief of which was the cathedral, closely rivalled
by the Liebfrauenkirche or Marienkirche (St Mary's). By the end
of the Thirty Years War and the Peace of Westphalia, Halle had
been assigned to Prussia. This arrangement, though, only came into
force with the death of Augustus, Duke of Saxe-Magdeburg, in
1680, just before Handel was born. The ducal court was then
removed to Saxe-Weissenfels, some forty miles from Halle.

During the reign of Duke Augustus, Halle had become a musical
centre of some importance, and had even seen the production of
German operas in the ducal Residence. During Handel's youth
there was still a number of musicians in the town, the most important
of whom was Friedrich Wilhelm Zachau (1663-1712), organist of
the Marienkirche. Before him, the most important of Halle's
musicians had been Samuel Scheidt (1587-1654), a composer of

7

international distinction. He and others had done much to give provincial Halle a rich musical life of its own, which centred to a large extent on the musical services of the various churches, but also included the city waits, or minstrels, and the music societies (*collegia musica*) which were so characteristic a feature of musical life in late seventeenth and early eighteenth century German university cities. In 1694 Halle became a university town when the Elector of Brandenburg gave permission for the old Ritter-Akademie to be changed into the University of Halle, soon to become famous as a centre of theological and legal studies. It was in this thriving and far from sleepy environment that Handel was to pass his youth. It is worth noting that Halle was a Protestant city; if Handel had been educated in a Roman Catholic environment his life and development would undoubtedly have been entirely different.

PARENTAGE AND EDUCATION

Georg Friedrich Händel (or George Frideric Handel as he is more commonly known in England) was born on February 23, 1685. His father, also named Georg, was an elderly barber-surgeon who, having already had one family by an early marriage, married again quite late in life, his second wife being Dorothea Taust, the daughter of a Lutheran pastor. Handel's father was a man of some distinction in Halle combining, perhaps rather curiously to modern thinking, the dual professions of barber and surgeon. In those days, however, when a great deal of surgery consisted of blood-letting, it was perhaps not at all surprising to find the two callings united. The elder Handel, a man of severe principles, held the appointment of barber-surgeon to the court of Saxe-Weissenfels, and it was during a visit to the court that his small son's musical propensities were discovered.

By the age of six or seven George Frideric had contrived to learn the clavichord; legend has it that this was achieved in spite of parental disapproval, by practising on a tiny instrument in the attic. It is hard to say whether there is any truth in this story, but the Duke did overhear the boy playing the organ in the court chapel at Weissenfels in about 1693, and thereupon urged on the father the desirability of having his son study music seriously. This

8

was apparently somewhat grudgingly allowed, perhaps more with a view to pleasing the Duke than to encouraging the son, for old Handel was determined that his son should pursue a legal and not a musical career. However, the boy was then placed with Friedrich Wilhelm Zachau, under whom he soon made rapid progress in music and studied composition, oboe and violin as well as harpsichord and organ. Zachau had a considerable library of music which held French, Italian and German scores, many of which Handel copied, and thereby became familiar with the current international trends in music. By the age of ten he was already beginning to compose fluently, and if the set of half-a-dozen trio sonatas for two oboes and bassoon actually were composed by him at that period, as is often claimed, then they show evidence of a musical precocity as great as that of the infant Mozart.

At this time, or possibly a little later, the boy was taken on a trip to Berlin, where he astonished the Prussian court with his playing. Despite this the father was still adamant that his son was to become a lawyer and not a musician, for the latter profession was not held in particularly high regard in late-seventeenth century Germany. When Handel was twelve his father died, leaving his widow with a youthful family of a son and two daughters. They were no doubt reasonably well provided for, their father having been a careful man. This, nevertheless, left them bereft of his stern direction. Though the father was dead, his influence remained, and so young Handel continued his legal, as well as his musical studies, and was eventually enrolled as a law student at the University. It was at about this time that he first met Georg Philipp Telemann, an exceptionally gifted young man some four years older than himself. Handel struck up a friendship with Telemann which lasted the rest of their lives, and which was maintained by correspondence during the periods when they did not actually meet each other.

When Handel entered Halle University, at the age of seventeen, he was already so highly regarded as a musician as to be appointed organist of the local cathedral. He is said to have composed a number of church cantatas at this time, but if this is so they seem to have disappeared, unless they are represented by some of the so-called Deutsche Arien—arias for solo voice with obbligato

9

melody instrument and continuo. In some ways these resemble some of the church cantatas of his friend Telemann.

Handel was not long at the University; the dry study of law no doubt had little attraction for him. Instead he travelled to Hamburg where there was a famous opera-house, the first of its kind in Germany. When Handel arrived in Hamburg, that famous ' Opera House on the Goose-Market ' was being directed by the celebrated Reinhard Keiser (1674-1739), Germany's first great opera-composer. Through the kind efforts of another gifted young man, Johann Mattheson (1681-1764), Handel obtained a post as a second violin in the opera orchestra. It was not long though before his outstanding ability as a continuo player was discovered and he was elevated to the important role of accompanist, or as it is called in Italian, ' Maestro al cembalo '. Mattheson, who later became a famous critic and writer on music, said of Handel at this time that he had a droll sense of humour, ' behaving as if he did not know how many beans made five ' with a knack of making humorous remarks with a completely serious face. This inevitably made even the gravest of people laugh, and was a trait which did not altogether desert him even during the troubled years of his later life. Whilst at Hamburg, Handel and his friend Mattheson took leave of absence to go to Lübeck, where the ageing organist and composer Dietrich (or Diderik) Buxtehude (1637-1707) was apparently thinking of retiring from his arduous duties as director of music to the city churches there. However, when the two young men arrived at Lübeck, they discovered that one of the conditions of succeeding to Buxtehude's position entailed marrying Buxtehude's daughter (presumably not in the first flower of youth) and so the two young men hastily returned to Hamburg. It is said that J S Bach also went to Lübeck on a similar errand and likewise beat as hurried a retreat.

A year or so after the Lübeck adventure, a quarrel broke out between Handel and Mattheson. The latter, who was not only a composer himself, but also a singer and player, had written an opera on the subject of Cleopatra, in which he sang the part of Mark Antony, a role which terminated half an hour or so before the opera itself ended. At that point, Mattheson liked to go down into the orchestra pit, seat himself at the director's harpsichord, and conduct the remainder of the opera. This seems to have irked Handel, and on one particular occasion he refused to budge from his seat. Both were incensed and when the opera was over the pair went into the Goose Market, drew swords, and actually began to fight an angry duel, surrounded and encouraged by the onlookers. As Mattheson himself wrote, in later years, the result might have been disastrous ' had not God's guidance graciously ordained that my blade, thrusting against the broad metallic coat button of my opponent, should be shattered '. (Not, be it noted, ' the friendly score ' which some authorities say intercepted Mattheson's blade—after all, it was Mattheson's sword and he should have known!) The two quickly forgave each other and Mattheson says that they were soon better friends than ever before. They were together at the rehearsals of Handel's first opera, *Almira,* in December 1704, which was followed by its triumphant performance the following January. A second opera, *Nero,* produced at Hamburg on February 25, 1705, was apparently a failure. Handel, though, was probably already dreaming of Italy, and sometime during that summer of 1705 he seems to have found an opportunity to visit that country, then the goal of all northern musicians' hopes and aspirations. How he got to Italy, or exactly when he arrived there, we do not really know. Mattheson, who later on seems to have grown rather jealous of Handel, says rather sneeringly that Handel ' had the opportunity of a free ride to Italy with von Binitz ', but as no one seems to know who Binitz was, this is not very helpful either. All that we do know is that by the end of 1706 Handel was already in Italy and taking the land by storm with his astonishing gifts as composer and performer. Never had the Italians heard such virtuosity in organ playing and even as a harpsichordist his only possible rival was the brilliant young Domenico Scarlatti (1685-1757), his close contemporary.

HANDEL IN ITALY

The exact details of Handel's journeyings are still somewhat obscure, in spite of the excellent work done recently by Ursula

Kirkendale on some of the Italian documents of the time, in which she has succeeded in clearing up many old misconceptions and misleading legends concerning Handel's Italian period. Even so, there are still many tantalising gaps in the records. We still have no very clear idea of what Handel did between summer 1705, when he is supposed to have left Hamburg for Italy, and his appearance at Rome in the spring of 1707. He apparently composed his Latin Psalm *Dixit Dominus* there, finishing it during April 1707, and his *Laudate pueri* and *Nisi Dominus* in the summer of that year. A little later we find him living first in the house of the Colonna family, and then in that of the great patron of music and art, Cardinal Pietro Ottoboni. Early in the next year he composed his magnificent Italian oratorio, *La Resurrezione* (The Resurrection) which was performed in the palace of the Marquis Francesco Maria Ruspoli on Easter Sunday, April 8, 1708. (There are extant in the Ruspoli accounts some very amusing items about the renting of bed and bedding for the composer.) By June 1708, Handel was in Naples where he composed his Italian serenata *Aci, Galatea e Polifemo* at the house of the Duke of Alvito. He also composed a number of Italian cantatas, presumably for performance at Naples. In the spring of 1709 he was in Siena, where his *Pianto di Maria* was performed by command of Prince Ferdinand of Medici. By December of that year he was in Venice, where his opera *Agrippina* was produced with much success during the Carnival.

Many and varied are the tales told about Handel in Italy—how young Domenico Scarlatti, finest of all Italian harpsichordists, crossed himself on overhearing Handel play the harpsichord, saying ' It is either the Devil or the Saxon '; of how the two became good friends, and had an amicable contest on organ and harpsichord, in which Handel triumphed at the organ, and Scarlatti at the harpsichord. One of the most enlightening of such stories concerns the great violinist-composer Arcangelo Corelli, who was directing a performance of (it is said) Handel's *Il trionfo del tempo e del disinganno* (The triumph of time and truth). Corelli did not lead off the overture with sufficient fire for Handel, who snatched fiddle and bow from the great man's hands and proceeded to show him how the passage should be played. ' Ma, caro Sassone ' protested

12

the gentle virtuoso, 'Questa musica é nel stylo Francese, di ch'io non m'intendo . . .' (But, dear Saxon, this music is in the French style, which I do not understand . . .). We do know for certain that Corelli did actually direct the orchestra in the Roman performance of Handel's oratorio *La resurrezione* mentioned above, and it is quite possible that he directed *Il trionfo* as well. Handel is reputed to have been much in demand at the meetings of the Arcadian societies which then existed in Italy. These were literary, artistic and musical gatherings in which the members were given the names of mythical shepherds and shepherdesses and the like. Handel never seems to have actually joined one of these clubs, and nothing is known of any Arcadian name he might have borne, but his great talents undoubtedly made him a welcome guest at such gatherings.

The important fact about Handel's Italian sojourn is not exactly what he did in Italy, or when he did it, but the total effect that Italy produced on him. He entered that country an almost untried 'prentice hand; he left it a world master. During his Italian travels he met and enjoyed the friendship of some of the world's greatest composers—Corelli, the two Scarlattis (Alessandro and Domenico) and that fascinating composer and diplomat, Agostino Steffani. When he left Italy to return to his native Germany, sometime during the summer of 1710, he was complete master of the Italian style of composition, the international language of music at that time. He was no longer a provincial North German composer; he was 'Signior Hendel', the composer of Italian music, and it was as such that he came northwards to take up residence in Hanover, as Kapellmeister to the Elector of that city. On the way to Hanover he stopped and dallied somewhat at an even more musical court, that of the Elector Johann Wilhelm of Dusseldorf, where he possibly renewed acquaintance with his older friend Steffani. Handel overstayed his leave of absence there so long that the Dusseldorf Elector and his consort were obliged to write letters to the Elector of Hanover, apologising for detaining him.

EARLY YEARS IN ENGLAND AND THE FIRST OPERAS

Hanover was too small and too provincial to hold Handel for long, and in the autumn of 1710 we find him on leave of absence again, this time bound for England, apparently at the invitation of various English friends, encountered no doubt in Italy.

In England, Handel found an interesting musical situation. There had been something of a vacuum in English musical life since the untimely death of Henry Purcell (1659-1695) some fifteen years before. None of that great man's musical heirs had the gifts necessary to succeed him, and the English type of opera which he had done so much to foster was already giving way to a polyglot, Anglo-Italian version of Italian opera, with singers of mixed nationalities singing in both languages, to the utter detriment of all stage illusion. Obviously London was ripe for true Italian opera, but without a great resident composer of such opera all remained confusion. Soon after Handel's arrival in London in the latter part of 1710, he was approached by Aaron Hill, the manager of the Queen's Theatre (thus named after Queen Anne, still then on the throne of England), concerning the possibility of his composing an Italian opera. A libretto was swiftly produced for him, written by Giacomo Rossi, the theatre poet, following a suggestion by Hill himself on the subject of Rinaldo, from Tasso's epic *Gerusalemme liberata* (Jerusalem set free). Handel set to work with a will and in a fortnight had the full score ready. With *Rinaldo,* produced in February 1711, Handel secured his British reputation for ever. *Rinaldo* was immediately successful, and John Walsh, the publisher, made so much money by printing the songs from it that Handel, in his typically dry way, suggested that next time Walsh should compose the opera and he, Handel, would publish it.

Handel was fêted and lionised everywhere, not only as a composer but also as a harpsichordist, for his performance in the theatre itself, and for his appearance at London concerts such as those of Thomas Britton, ' the musical small-coals ' man '. Britton was a fascinating character. He made his living by selling sacks of small coal, which he carried round on his own back during the daytime, at night turning his attention to music, his major passion. In his rather dingy rooms, entered by a rickety staircase, he gave concerts of chamber music which were frequented by all classes of music lovers, including some of the most distinguished people and greatest masters then in London, Handel amongst them. Britton

14

had a splendid library of music which was sold after his death; details of it can be found in the pages of Sir John Hawkins' *History of music*.

Handel, however lionised he might be in London, could not entirely forget that he was really in the service of the Elector of Hanover, and so back to Hanover he had perforce to go, returning there via Dusseldorf and Halle, where he visited his widowed mother, and once more saw his elder sister, Dorothea, now married to a lawyer, Dr M D Michaelson. His younger sister Johanna Christiana had died at Halle at the age of nineteen, some two years before. He stayed in Hanover for about a year, then once more requested leave of absence to return to England, where they were clamouring for further operas from his pen. He was allowed to go, provided he returned ' in a reasonable time '—a phrase which he interpreted in rather an elastic fashion. In London he produced his opera *Il Pastor fido* (The faithful shepherd) on November 22, 1712, and composed another, *Teseo* (Theseus) for production early in the New Year. Unfortunately the manager, one Sweeney or MacSwiney, absconded with the box-office takings, leaving every-one unpaid, but the cast continued to run the opera house them-selves.

Handel now attempted the difficult task, for a foreigner, of setting English words to music, and composed a splendid Te Deum to celebrate the Peace of Utrecht, modelling it to some extent on Purcellian patterns. He also composed a charming ode for the birth-day of Queen Anne (February 6), a piece which pleased the Queen sufficiently for her to request Handel to hurry and finish his grand *Te Deum* and *Jubilate* in time for it to be performed at the peace celebrations in St Paul's Cathedral on July 7, 1713. Although the Queen was an ailing woman and could not herself attend the cathedral ceremony, she had the music repeated privately and was so satisfied with it that she awarded Handel a pension of £200 per annum, an award which was continued and later augmented by her successors, and which was to stand Handel in very good stead in some of his future financial straits.

Handel's English prestige was now immense; to the English music-lovers of the Augustan age he was not merely a good composer, but *the* composer, the greatest that had ever lived. Addison and Steele might sneer in the pages of *The spectator* at the absurdities they found in the Italian opera, but to the aristocratic throng it was irrelevant. Italian opera was the fashion and they flocked to it, and voted young Mr Handel the greatest master of all time—for the moment. Handel himself was *persona grata* in the houses of the nobility and it is said that he actually lived at the house of the Earl of Burlington, in Piccadilly, always a centre for all kinds of artists, writers and musicians. It was probably there that Handel met such eminent literary figures as Pope, Gay, Arbuthnot and so on. His opera *Silla* (Sulla) is said to have been produced at Burlington House.

It is perhaps worth while at this point to discuss the typical opera seria which Handel wrote for the London stage. Italian opera at that time was in many ways indeed the ' exotic and irrational entertainment ' of Dr Johnson's famous definition. It was primarily ' singers' opera ', with the emphasis placed very much on the solo arias warbled by the famous Italian castrati singers such as Senesino, Farinelli and their like. The fantastic artificial voices were produced in Italy by the castration of likely boy singers, thus prolonging their treble voices at the expense of losing their masculinity. There were female sopranos as well, of course, and they vied with the petted and pampered male sopranos and contraltos for the favour of the aristocratic audiences who were the main supporters of Italian opera in all the countries of Europe. So jealous of each other were the singers that great care had to be taken by librettist and composer alike to see that each singer had his or her due number of arias, with sufficiently effective entries and exits to produce the applause on which they doted. The stories on which the operas were founded were artificial in the extreme, usually taken from ancient mythology or legend, and full of plots and counterplots, guisings and double disguisings, so that they would be hard enough to unravel, even in a language which the audience might understand, much less a foreign tongue. But this form, for all its artificiality obviously fascinated Handel and he devoted a great deal of his artistic career to composing and producing Italian operas.

While still in England he may have heard with some dismay, in August, 1714, that Queen Anne, his patroness, had died and that

16

his erstwhile master George, the Elector of Hanover, was now King of England. I say 'may have', because it is not beyond the bounds of possibility that Handel had been deliberately allowed to overstay his leave in England as a discreet observer of the local scene. After all his friend Agostino Steffani had been diplomat as well as composer at the court of Dusseldorf. It was believed that Handel, fearing the wrath of his royal master, composed the *Water Music* to placate him. All the evidence, though, seems to show that Handel did not compose the *Water Music* until some years later, and then only at the suggestion of Baron Kielmansegg, not of his own volition. In any case, he must have been at peace with the King by September 28, 1714, as on that Sunday morning we are told 'His Majesty went to his Royall Chappel at St James's . . . where *Te Deum* was sung, composed by Mr Handel . . . '.

Still busy with Italian opera, Handel produced his *Amadigi* (Amadis) during the May of 1715. In July, 1716, he went with the King to Hanover and took the opportunity to visit Dresden in search of singers for the London opera. He also revisited Hamburg (to meet Mattheson again, perhaps?) and went to see his family once more in Halle. He also seems to have persuaded an old acquaintance, Johann Christoph Schmidt, of Ansbach, to go to London, where as John Christopher Smith, senior, he became Handel's chief scribe and amanuensis. Back in London, he revived both *Rinaldo* and *Amadigi,* but the London opera house was in one of its recurrent fits of depression that it seemed unlikely to overcome for the moment. It was at about this time that the famous *Water Music* was performed at a royal water party on the Thames. One of the best accounts of the affair was written by Bonet, the Prussian resident in London, on July 19 (30), 1717, and sent home by him to the authorities in Berlin:

'A few weeks ago the King expressed to Baron Kilmanseck his desire to have a concert on the river, by subscription, similar to the masquerades this winter which the King never failed to attend. The Baron accordingly applied to Heidegger—a Swiss by origin, but the cleverest purveyor of entertainments to the Nobility. The latter replied that, much as he would wish to comply to His Majesty's desires, he must reserve subscriptions for the great events, namely

17

the masquerades, each of which brings him three or 400 guineas net. Observing His Majesty's chagrin at these difficulties, M. de Kilmanseck undertook to provide the concert on the river at his own expense. The necessary orders were given and the entertainment took place the day before yesterday. About eight in the evening the King repaired to his barge, into which were admitted the Duchess of Bolton, Countess Godolphin, Mad. de Kilmanseck, Mrs Were and the Earl of Orkney, the Gentleman of the Bedchamber in Waiting. Next to the King's barge was that of the musicians, about 50 in number, who played on all kinds of instruments, to wit trumpets, horns, hautboys, bassoons, German flutes, French flutes, violins and basses; but there were no singers. The music had been specially composed by the famous Handel, a native of Halle and His Majesty's principal Court Composer. His Majesty approved of it so greatly that he caused it to be repeated three times in all, although each performance lasted an hour—namely twice before and once after supper. The evening was all that could be desired for the festivity, the number of barges and above all of boats filled with people desirous of hearing was beyond counting; . . .'.

' PRINCELY CHANDOS '

It seems from this account, and others in the same vein, that the *Water Music* really was composed for this royal water frolic on the Thames, in July 1717, and not for some earlier occasion. About this time, however, another strong influence was to come into Handel's life. During the following September James Brydges, Earl of Carnarvon, wrote to a mutual friend, Dr John Arbuthnot: ' Mr Hendle has made me two new Anthems, very noble ones, & most think they exceed the two first: he is at work for 2 more and some Overtures to be plaied before the first Lesson. You had as good take Cannons in your way to London . . .'. This is the first intimation we have of the connection between Handel and that resplendent character James Brydges, later Duke of Chandos. Brydges had been Paymaster-General to the forces during the time of Marlborough's wars and, like most powerful officials of that era, had no doubt contrived to syphon off a good deal of public money into his own coffers. He lived in a very grand style on the proceeds, and

18

became a byword for ostentation, attended as he was on his journeyings by a small army of flamboyantly dressed retainers. Brydges was
also in the process of building himself a large and luxurious house
at Canons Park, near Edgware in Middlesex. He largely rebuilt the
local parish church of St Lawrence's, Whitchurch (or Little Stanmore) for use as a private chapel, until such time as the one in his
great house was ready.

It was at Canons Park that John Christopher Pepusch, his German-
born music director, later famous as arranger of the music for Gay's
Beggar's opera, directed the Earl's small but efficient musical establishment in the performance of surprisingly large-scale anthems.
Somehow—we still do not know exactly how, why or when—
Brydges persuaded Handel to become composer-in-residence at
Canons. He did not apparently displace Pepusch as musical director;
his particular task seeming to have been simply the composition and
performance of his own music. This consisted of anthems for performance in the chapel and some astonishing secular works which
were presumably performed in the house itself. Thus originated
not only the magnificent Chandos anthems, but also that inimitable
little masterpiece, the English masque or serenata of *Acis and
Galatea,* an achievement as uniquely immortal, in its own way, as
Messiah was to be later.

Another work of this period which was to have even more important future significance was a so-called masque, the semi-sacred
work *Haman and Mordecai,* which later became transformed into
the first of Handel's English oratorios, *Esther.* It would be fascinating to know exactly how such a work as *Acis and Galatea* was
performed at Canons, and to see the room in which it was first
heard, but the great house was demolished in 1744, soon after the
Duke of Chandos's death. All that has survived of the scenes of
Handel's triumphs is the parish church of St Lawrence, where he
must have directed the majority of his Chandos anthems since the
Duke's private chapel was not opened until 1720, by which time
Handel was no longer in his service. It is often conjectured that
Acis and Galatea was performed chamber music fashion, with per-
haps only five singers and a tiny instrumental ensemble to match.
We shall never know for sure, because in later years *Acis* surprised

its composer by flowering into a work for much larger forces, so that what had been written for an aristocrat's private delectation became the delight of the general public.

Legend tends to grow around such a figure as Handel, and one particular legend has grown around his residence at Canons, so that no one would have been more surprised than Handel himself at what posterity imagined of him. In about 1720 he published a collection of harpsichord pieces, the celebrated *Suites de pièces pour le clavecin*. The fourth of these suites contains a charming air with a set of variations and it is from this air, a hundred years or so later, that the legend grew. For some unknown reason this tune became known in the early nineteenth century as ' The harmonious blacksmith '. Fable, having produced the nickname, had to produce a blacksmith, one William Powell, to go with it. Then, of course, a just-so story to account for his association with the tune had to be provided. The story which was eventually put forward was that Handel, caught in a violent thunderstorm, sheltered in Powell's forge at Edgware and was fascinated by his anvil, which gave forth two notes when he struck it. On these, it was claimed, Handel founded his tune. What is more, the original anvil was said to have been rediscovered in a local junk-yard, as a piece of ' corroborative verisimilitude '. The whole tale was a complete fabrication of course, but once told it persisted, so much so that we still call Handel's air ' The harmonious blacksmith ' and no doubt will continue to do so despite the fact that no one would have been more surprised (perhaps annoyed!) than Handel himself to have it thus labelled.

THE FIRST ROYAL ACADEMY OF MUSIC

Handel was impatient to return to Italian opera and had already been over on the Continent in search of Italian singers to help form a new company, under the direction of the Swiss, Heidegger, charmingly described as ' the ugliest man in London ', whom we have already encountered in connection with the *Water music*. This new venture was christened the Royal Academy of Music though it was nothing to do with the present teaching establishment of that name. The title was derived from the French opera, known as the Académie Royale de la Musique, founded in Lully's time. For the new London establishment, Handel produced his latest opera, *Radamisto,* at the King's Theatre in the Haymarket on April 27, 1720. It was an ominous year, though, to be starting an operatic venture; the year of the notorious South Sea Bubble, when financial madness seized London and many an innocent person lost everything in the wild speculations of the day. Handel himself dabbled in stocks and shares, as did everyone else, but he was shrewd and seems to have escaped the fate of some of his contemporaries. By September the worst was over; the stocks began to rise again, and public confidence returned.

Meanwhile the directors of the new opera had begun to negotiate with the veteran Italian composer Giovanni Bononcini (1670-1755) to come to London and compose for them. He arrived in England towards the end of 1720, and so began the first of those operatic rivalries which were to bedevil Handel for the next twenty years or so. There was nothing that eighteenth century opera devotees loved more than a rivalry of some kind, either between singers or composers, and Handel suffered greatly from this during his years as an opera composer. The factions were already rising high early in 1721 when London's opera going public was regaled with the production of a tripartite opera called *Muzio Scevola,* on April 15. The first act was by one Filippo Mattei (otherwise known as ' Pippo '), the second by Bononcini and the third by Handel. ' Pippo ' was of little account, but Bononcini had a great reputation, and being an Italian was much preferred by many noble patrons to the Saxon Handel. However some down-to-earth Englishmen, such as the Lancashire wit John Byrom, could see little difference between the two—how was he to know that in the course of the next hundred years or so, his 'Mynheer Handel' was to become the darling of singers in Lancashire? Byrom penned a famous and witty epigram :

Some say, compar'd to Bononcini,
That Mynheer Handel's but a ninny;
Others aver, that he to Handel
Is scarcely fit to hold a Candle :
Strange that this Difference there should be
'Twixt Tweedle-dum and Tweedle-dee!

Byrom can be forgiven, even by Handelians; the world would be

21

that much poorer without his amusing *jeu d'esprit*. He was not very musical and there seemed really very little to choose between the two protagonists, as composers of Italian opera.

Handel's true greatness was to come later and in an area still unsuspected, even by his greatest admirers. On the whole, his operatic style was more solid than that of his Italian rivals—he had more ' science ', as his contemporaries would have said. If anything, this gave his rivals an advantage with a pleasure-bent public. However, opposition of any kind always seems to have increased Handel's native stubborness, and it was to be many a long year before he relinquished his fickle mistress, the Italian opera. Newer and even more brilliant singers were now gracing the London stage— Senesino, the great alto, Signora Durastanti, the soprano, and Boschi, the bass, were now contending for the favours of the London public. Senesino and Boschi both appeared in Handel's next opera, *Floridante* (produced on December 9, 1721).

Little is known of Handel's activities during the year 1722, except that towards the end of it he composed the opera *Ottone* (Otho) This was performed on January 12, 1722, and achieved immortality through the gavotte in its overture, which later became one of the most popular of all Handel's melodies, known as ' the Gavotte in Otho '. The production of *Ottone* had been delayed to await the arrival of yet another famous singer, the soprano Francesca Cuzzoni (known somewhat unkindly as ' The Pig ', on account of her not exactly beautiful features). Homely or not, Cuzzoni was a superb singer. She was also a typical prima donna and behaved accordingly, although she met her match in Handel, whose ' great bear ' of a temper was so aroused one day that he snatched her up by the waist and threatened to pitch her out of the window, shouting: ' Madame, they say you are a very devil; know then that I am Beelzebub, the Prince of Devils . . .'. This is often related as an example of his peremptory temper, but it may only have been an outburst of his rough Polyphemus-like sense of humour, which was apt to be a bit boisterous at times.

Ottone proved very popular, but the next Handel opera, *Flavio* (Flavius), produced in May, 1723, was less well received. By this time yet another Italian composer had arrived on the scene. This was the veteran Attilio Ariosti (b. 1666), a kind and gentle soul, ill suited to the intrigues and rivalries of the opera house. He had little success in England, although his music has great charm. His *Vespasiano* (Vespasian) (January 14, 1724) was a resounding failure. Handel came to the rescue with one of his greatest operas, *Giulio Cesare* (Julius Caesar) performed on February 20, 1724, and which was a great success, remaining so for many years. It has been equally successful in modern times, and has been one of the most often revived of all his operas. (One cannot help wondering what the rather plain Cuzzoni looked like as the seductive Cleopatra!)

Handel followed *Giulio Cesare* at the end of the year with another fine opera, *Tamerlano* (Tamburlaine) and then, in the new year, with another of his great successes, *Rodelinda,* produced in the February of 1725. A year or so later came *Scipione* (Scipio), best remembered for its march, which became immensely popular after widespread use by the Guards. Then came *Alessandro* (Alexander) on 5 May, 1726 in which another great soprano, Faustina Bordoni, came into rivalry with Cuzzoni. Faustina, however, was as beautiful as Cuzzoni was plain, and in later years became the wife of another eminent Saxon composer, Johann Adolf Hasse, music-director at Dresden. But however charming Faustina may have been, she was not prepared to yield to Cuzzoni, and so more trouble was heaped upon the unfortunate Handel's head in order to balance the rival claims of the two prime donne. The directors of the Academy were very well pleased with Handel's next opera, *Admeto* (Admetus) (which made its first appearance in January, 1727) but still continued in the practice of contracting three rival composers, Handel, Ariosti and Bononcini, to compose operas in rotation. No doubt they knew the value of such rivalries in boosting the box office receipts. Not long after the production of *Admeto* Handel applied for papers of naturalisation and accordingly took the oath of allegiance as George Frideric Handel, becoming a British subject with the King's consent on February 20. It was one of King George I's last public acts; a few months later Handel was composing the music for his successor's coronation, which took place on October 11, 1727, and is now chiefly remembered because of Handel's music, and particularly for that most famous of all coronation anthems, *Zadok the Priest,* which has been heard at the coronation ceremonies of practically every British monarch since.

Handel's new opera, *Riccardo primo* (Richard the first), was produced in the November of that year, and he followed it with two more new works: *Siroe* on February 17, 1728 and *Tolomeo* (Ptolemy) on April 30. Italian opera, though, was once again in the doldrums and everyone was flocking to see John Gay's *Beggar's opera* instead, which had been produced at the theatre in Lincoln's Inn Fields on January 29, 1728. Its audacious libretto and wealth of catchy tunes, arranged by Handel's old acquaintance Dr Pepusch, gave it an immediate popularity which it has maintained ever since. The *Beggar's opera* is often held to be a satire on Handelian opera, but it is in a different *genre,* and owed its initial success more to being a satire on the Prime Minister, Sir Robert Walpole, than to any fancied connection with Italian opera.

THE SECOND ROYAL ACADEMY

The first Royal Academy of Music had now collapsed but, nothing daunted, Handel set out to form another, going to Italy to book fresh singers, and calling at Halle on the way back to see his now aged and infirm mother. The new Royal Academy of Music opened its doors with the production of Handel's latest opera, *Lotario,* on December 2, 1729, but it was not a great success. He followed it with *Partenope* in February, 1730, and then turned to revivals of *Tolomeo* and *Scipione.* A new opera, *Poro* (Porus), based on Metastasio's *Alessandro in India,* followed in February, 1731. Much more significant were a stage performance of *Acis and Galatea,* given at John Rich's theatre in Lincoln's Inn Fields in March, and followed a year or so later by the English oratorio *Esther,* derived from another old Canons-period work, the masque of *Haman and Mordecai,* which was now produced in honour of Handel's birthday, February 23. This production, directed by Bernard Gates, Master of the Children of the Chapel Royal, was followed by two public performances, one of these being at the King's Theatre under Handel's own direction. Although he probably did not realise it, destiny was already edging Handel along in the direction he must eventually go.

Meanwhile he was still deeply involved with Italian opera. His *Ezio* and *Sosarme* were produced early in 1732, and he composed another opera, *Orlando,* for production in early 1733. Significantly enough he had also composed another oratorio, *Deborah,* to words by Samuel Humphreys which he put on at the King's Theatre in March, 1733, with a largely Italian cast—their English diction must have been incredible! Senesino sang in *Deborah,* but a little later forsook Handel to join forces with various aristocratic patrons to set up a rival opera in the Lincoln's Inn Fields, called 'The Opera of the Nobility', with Nicola Porpora (1686-1766) as composer. That gossipy periodical, *The Bee,* gleefully commented on the situation: 'We are credibly informed that one Day last Week, Mr H–d–l, Director-General of the Opera-House, sent a Message to Signor Senesino, the famous Italian Singer, acquainting Him, that he had no farther Occasion for his Service: and that Senesino replied, the next Day, by a Letter, containing a full Resignation of all his Parts in the Opera, which he had performed for many Years with great Applause . . . the World seems greatly ASTONISH'D at so unexpected an Event, and all true Lovers of Musick GRIEVE to see so fine a Singer dismissed, in so critical a Conjecture'. Whether Handel really sacked Senesino, or whether the latter handed his resignation in first, we do not know, but obviously the scene was now set for another of those bitter operatic rivalries which no doubt delighted many of the patrons, although it must have disgusted many a true music-lover. The position was acerbated by the quarrel between the King and his son Frederick, Prince of Wales, who opposed Handel simply because his father favoured him.

HANDEL IN OXFORD
In the summer of 1733 Handel achieved a success greater than anything so far vouchsafed him by the Opera House; he was invited to go to Oxford to provide the music for the Oxford Encaenia or 'Music Act' of that year, and in accepting turned it into a regular Handel Festival, much to the annoyance of some of the pro-Jacobite dons, who sneeringly referred to 'Handel and his lousy crew of foreign fiddlers'. But the general public was not so particular; Oxford was crowded out with company, and Handel enjoyed

very full houses for everything he produced there. Between July 6 and 14 Handel performed *Esther, Deborah,* his *Te Deum,* some anthems, and a new oratorio, called *Athaliah.* He also now began his custom of playing organ concertos ' between the acts ' of his oratorios. Altogether he went back to London a much richer man than he left it, but without the degree of Doctor of Music which he is said to have been offered. Later that same year, he went away again to Italy to engage new singers (including the popular Carestini) to replace those who had left with Senesino. He also managed to forestall the rival company to some extent by opening before they were ready, but his own new opera *Arianna* (Ariadne) was not produced until January 1734. That year was especially significant in court circles due to the marriage of Princess Anne with the Prince of Orange on March 14. To celebrate the event Handel composed an Italian serenata called *Parnasso in Festa* (Festival on Parnassus), which was produced at the King's Theatre on March 13, with the Royal Family, including the betrothed couple, in attendance. At the wedding ceremony next day, at St. James's, an especially written wedding anthem to the words ' This is the day the Lord hath made ' was sung ' by a great number of voices and instruments '. Both these works were of the pasticcio variety, hurriedly put together for the occasion, but both highly successful. The same was true of a set of six concertos, some of which were played during the wedding festivities, and which were assembled with others to make up the set of six published later that year by Walsh as the six Concerti Grossi, op 3. These became popularly known as the ' Hautboy Concertos ', from the prominent parts allotted to those instruments. Handel also re-wrote an old failure, *Il Pastor fido* (first produced in 1712) and performed it at Covent Garden, having come to an agreement with John Rich, the new proprietor of the theatre which was to become increasingly important to Handel as the years went by.

TERPSICHOREAN INTERLUDE

A new attraction now appeared at Covent Garden in the seductive form of the French danseuse Mlle Marie Sallé, who had originally appeared in London in 1717 as a child prodigy and now returned to make her reappearance as an adult dancer. Handel was to compose some of his most enchanting music for La Sallé, in the ballets which he inserted into the scores of his next operas. He set a prologue, called *Terpsicore*, in which she danced the title role, to precede the re-written *Pastor fido II*, produced in this new form at Covent Garden in November 1734. This performance was also notable for the first appearance of the English tenor, John Beard, in the first of the Handel roles which he was later to make so memorable. Handel followed *Terpsicore* and *Pastor fido II* with two further operas emphasising both chorus and ballet; *Ariodante* (January 1735), and one of his finest masterpieces, *Alcina* (April 1735). Meanwhile he had revived *Athaliah* (also during that April) along with some of his organ concertos, a form new to England, if not the whole musical world.

Both theatres were doing badly, however, and it seemed that no attraction could keep one opera house prosperous, much less two. For the next year Handel turned once more towards music composed to English words, and in February produced his setting of Dryden's old Cecilian ode, *Alexander's Feast*. It was a great success; the London *Daily post* the next day reported that 'Never was upon the like Occasion so numerous and splendid an Audience at any Theatre in London, there being at least 1300 Persons present...'.

Handel, whose general and financial worries had brought him near to physical and nervous breakdown by the end of the previous season, was triumphantly vindicated. He now composed a wedding anthem for the marriage of the Prince of Wales and a festive opera, *Atalanta*, performed at Covent Garden in May 1736. Two new operas were composed during the autumn for production during the next season, in which he had as rival, at the other house, the popular composer Johann Adolph Hasse (1699-1783), another 'beloved Saxon', but some fourteen years younger and consequently more 'modern' in composition. The new year, 1737, saw the production of the next two Handel operas: *Arminio* (January) and *Giustino* (February).

FROM OPERA TO ORATORIO

A fresh pattern of life now began to emerge for Handel as an

27

alternative to his earlier sole reliance on Italian opera. The success of *Alexander's feast* was obviously causing his thoughts to veer in the direction of works using English words, and in 1737 he gave another Lenten oratorio season which included revivals of *Esther, Alexander's feast* and a new version of his early Italian oratorio, *Il trionfo del tempo.* But he was worn out by work and worry, and suffered a severe paralytic stroke. However, he managed to get to the baths at Aix-la-Chapelle, where the treatment worked wonders for him, and he went back to London a giant refreshed, in the following November, to write a fine funeral anthem, *The ways of Zion do mourn,* for his patroness Queen Caroline, whose obsequies took place in Westminster Abbey on December 17, 1737. His old acquaintance Heidegger, who had collected together the remnants of the two companies (for Handel's rivals had fared as badly as or even worse than himself), opened again at the King's Theatre and commissioned Handel to compose two new operas for him, to be produced in the following year, 1738. Handel complied, and besides composing *Faramondo,* arranged a pasticcio, *Alessandro Severo* (Alexander Severus). *Faramando* was produced in January 1738, and *Alessandro Severo* in February. A little later came *Serse* (Xerxes) (in April), Handel's one and only comic opera which, it must be admitted, is not really very funny, being more notable for its opening number, the famous so-called ' Largo '—actually the aria ' Ombra mai fu '. Handel had a lively enough sense of humour, but it was usually at its best when it worked subconsciously.

In the latter part of 1738 he wrote two of his finest English works: *Saul* (to a libretto by Charles Jennens, the Leicestershire landowner who was later to become more famous for his work on the text of *Messiah*) and the strongly choral oratorio *Israel in Egypt,* to words from the Old Testament usually supposed to have been selected by Handel himself. That same year Walsh published the highly popular Six Organ Concertos, op 4. *Saul* was produced at the King's Theatre during 1739, and *Israel* in the following April. The former was reasonably successful, the latter was not. It was one of the great disappointments of Handel's life that *Israel in Egypt* never really succeeded—he is even said to have threatened to destroy his score. But eighteenth century taste ran more towards solo arias than large-scale choruses, and it must be admitted that this is an unbalanced work, with its strong emphasis on the chorus. It is also a work which shows Handel's practice of ' borrowing ' from earlier composers, the music being largely reworked from a seventeenth century serenata by Alessandro Stradella. This propensity of Handel's was always most in evidence at times of stress and worry, and it is obvious again in his setting of another Dryden *Ode on St Cecilia's Day,* which Handel finished on September 24, 1739. He immediately went on to compose the twelve superb Concerti Grossi for strings, published later as his op 6. The ode was performed with some success on St Cecilia's Day, 1739, the concertos being written partly for performance during that season and partly with a view to publication the following year. The season of 1739-40 saw also the composition and production of another masterpiece, Handel's magnificent setting of Milton's *L'Allegro ed il penseroso,* with words arranged by Jennens, who characteristically added a third part of his own with the typical Georgian title of *Il moderato.* The complete work was first performed at the theatre in Lincoln's Inn Fields in February 1740 and has always proved a leading favourite among Handel's English works, for its matchless combination of superb poetry with equally splendid music.

Handel, for all his experimentation with English word-setting, still had not entirely abandoned the Italian opera, and he composed two further examples in that *genre.* The first, *Imeneo* (Hymen), was produced on St Cecilia's Day, 1740, and his very last, *Deidamia,* in January, 1741. The latter was a failure, and with it he finally abandoned Italian opera. He had devoted the best years of his life to Italian opera seria, and was rewarded with more worry than pleasure, more pain than profit. Yet he obviously loved Italian opera, for all its absurdities. It is clear that he only abandoned it with great reluctance and after many difficulties, when it became patent, even to him, that the public really wanted no more of his operas. Only then did he finally turn to that which was to prove his ultimate salvation, the English oratorio. Meanwhile, his twelve Concerti Grossi or Grand Concertos, op 6, were published that same season by Walsh. To us, these twelve concertos represent the summit of Baroque orchestral composition, to be ranked only with

29

Corelli's op 6 and Bach's Brandenburg Concertos. It is strange to read Sir John Hawkins' comment on the op 6 set, in his *History of music,* that ' the composition of music merely instrumental, and of many parts, was not Handel's greatest excellence '.

Since Handel's finances were once more under severe strain he renounced public appearances and devoted himself to composition. During the summer of 1741 he received from Jennens the word-book of a new oratorio, with words selected from the Old and New Testament, on the subject of the Messiah. Handel seems to have realised its possibilities immediately and set to work on it in a fever of inspiration on August 22, finishing it on September 12—about three weeks in all—surely a record for the production of one of the world's greatest masterpieces. Not content with that, he immediately turned his attention to another libretto, sent to him by his friend Newburgh Hamilton, and taken from Milton's *Samson Agonistes,* which he set in about a month, the result being another splendid masterpiece. Handel's creative powers, at the age of fifty six or so, were obviously running at their highest. There is very little evidence of plagiarism in either work, except for some passages in the overture to *Samson,* and some self-borrowing in the case of *Messiah.*

HANDEL'S BORROWINGS

It is perhaps worth while to pause at this moment, with Handel on the verge of one of his very greatest triumphs, to consider the vexed question of his purloining other people's music and making it his own, by right of conquest, as it were. That he did this again and again has been abundantly proven; one cannot attempt to explain away what are obvious plagiarisms, some large, some small, but all quite undoubted, by pretending that Handel was not aware of what he was doing. He must have known, in some of these instances at least, that he was literally stealing other men's ideas. One of the chief sufferers in this respect was his old friend Telemann, from whose *Musique de table* (published in 1733) Handel borrowed many a theme, and sometimes even whole movements. Similarly with Gottlieb Muffat's *Componimenti musicali,* a set of harpsichord lessons, from which Handel consistently purloined themes and even complete pieces, such as the March in *Joshua,* originally the rigaudon in Muffat's first suite.

In Handel's defence we can urge that historically speaking he appeared at the end of a long period of development in which musical copyright was not only difficult to enforce, but was openly flouted in the forms of parody mass and pasticcio opera. At the same time one must remember that his rival Bononcini had been hounded out of England because of his supposed passing-off of a madrigal by Antonio Lotti as his own composition. That Handel did resort to borrowing is undeniable. Even his great admirer Dr Boyce admitted that Handel ' polished other men's pebbles into diamonds '. The most charitable explanation is that which was put forward by E J Dent, that Handel's most serious plagiarisms always occurred when he was under severe mental and nervous strain, particularly as he got older, and when he found it difficult to actually start a composition. Once an opening gambit was borrowed he was off, with his superb technique carrying him on, until the passage was finished. That he usually (but not always) improved on what he borrowed is rather beside the point; what must be admitted is that he did borrow, on a larger scale than any other major composer. But in the process he had the uncanny knack of making what he borrowed so completely his own that, without the necessary clues, no one would suspect the music of being anything but true Handel. Certainly a most puzzling case, and one that Handelians will go on arguing about for many years to come.

DUBLIN AND MESSIAH

Sometime during 1741 Handel apparently received an invitation from the Lord Lieutenant of Ireland to go over to Dublin and direct his music there. Whether he received that invitation before he started work on *Messiah* we shall probably never know; what is certain is that when he finally set off for Ireland, in the late Autumn of 1741, he had the *Messiah* score with him, ready for performance. On the way he stopped at Chester, waiting for a favourable wind to take his packet-boat across the stormy St George's Channel. There the future Dr Burney saw him, smoking his pipe at his inn. Thence, too, comes one of the most lovable of all Handelian stories, related by Burney himself. According to Burney, Handel had had the chorus parts of *Messiah* copied out before he left London, ready to be used in Ireland. Like many other musicians, Handel thought that the easiest way to check them was to get together a group of good sight-readers to sing through them. Among the singers was one Janson, a printer, who got on well enough until he came to the awkward chromatic passage in 'And with His stripes we are healed', when he failed miserably and broke down. 'You tog!' roared Handel, in his usual broken English, 'You tog! Did you not tell me dat you could sing at sight?' 'Aye, but not at first sight!' grumbled Janson, and so passed into immortality as the man who dared to answer back the great Mr Handel, who no doubt roared with laughter as promptly as he had with rage—Handel's passions were as quickly mollified as they were raised.

Arriving in Dublin, Handel opened a subscription for a series of concerts which included a performance of *L'Allegro, il penseroso ed il moderato*. It was highly successful and he wrote back home to Jennens in the following glowing terms:

Dublin, Decembr. 29. 1741.

S^r

it was with the greatest Pleasure I saw the Continuation of Your Kindness by the Lines You was pleased to send me, in Order to be prefix'd to your Oratorio Messiah, which I set to Musick before I left England. I am emboldned, Sir, by the generous Concern You please to take in relation to my affairs, to give You an Account of the Success I have met here. The Nobility did me the Honour to make amongst themselves a Subscription for 6 Nights, which did fill a Room of 600 Persons, so that I needed not sell one single Ticket at the Door, and without Vanity the Performance was received with general Approbation. Sigra. Avolio, which I brought with me from London pleases extraordinary, I have form'd an other Tenor Voice which gives great Satisfaction, the Basses and Counter Tenors are very good, and the rest of the Chorus Singers (by my Direction) do exceedingly well, as for the Instruments they are really excellent, Mr Dubourgh beeng at the Head of them, and the Musick sounds delightfully in this charming Room, which puts me in such Spirits (and my Health being so good) that I exert myself

32

on my Organ with more than usual success. I opened with the Allegro, Penseroso, & Moderato and I assure you that the Words of the Moderato are vastly admired. The Audience being composed (besides the Flower of Ladyes of Distinction and other People of the greatest Quality) of so many Bishops, Deans, Heads of the Colledge [*ie* Trinity College] the most eminent People in the Law as the Chancellor, Auditor General, &c., all of which are much taken with the Poetry. So that I am desired to perform it again the next time. I cannot sufficiently express the kind treatment I received here, but the Politeness of this generous Nation cannot be unknown to You, so I let You judge of the satisfaction I enjoy, passing my time with Honnour, profit and pleasure...

Handel was obviously enjoying himself. The ' charming room ' was the New Music Hall in Fishamble Street, where he was to put on the first performance of *Messiah*. But he did not hurry it; he kept it in reserve until the very end of his Dublin season, when his ensemble was really well-trained and ready to give a truly first-rate performance. He finally announced it as a charity performance on April 12, 1742, with a public rehearsal on April 9. The rehearsal took place, with immense *éclat;* Faulkner's *Dublin Journal* reported on April 10 that 'Yesterday Mr Handell's new Grand Sacred Oratorio, called, The MESSIAH, was rehearsed ... to a most Grand, Polite and crouded Audience; and was performed so well, that it gave universal Satisfaction to all present; and was allowed by the greatest Judges to be the finest Composition of Musick that was ever heard, and the sacred Words as properly adapted for the Occasion. N.B. At the Desire of several Persons of Distinction, the above Performance is put off to Tuesday next [the 13th]. The Doors will be opened at Eleven and the Performance begin at Twelve. Many Ladies and Gentlemen who are well-wishers to this Noble and Grand Charity for which this Oratorio is composed, request it as a Favour, that the Ladies who honour this Performance with their Presence would be pleased to come without Hoops (to their dresses), as it will greatly encrease the Charity, by making Room for more Company.' In another advertisement, the gentlemen were also requested to come ' without their swords '.

One very interesting point about this press statement is that it appears to claim that *Messiah* was really written with the deliberate intention of being performed for 'this Noble and Grand Charity'. In fact, three charitable causes were involved; the relief of the prisoners in the Dublin gaols; the support of Mercer's Hospital, and the Charitable Infirmary at the Inns Quay. From the beginning, Handel himself made very little personal profit from *Messiah;* it was nearly always performed by him for some charitable cause or other. After the actual performance, *Faulkner's Journal* was even more rhapsodic: 'On Tuesday last Mr Handel's Sacred Grand Oratorio, the MESSIAH, was performed at the New Musick-Hall in Fishamble-street; the best Judges allow it to be the most finished piece of Musick. Words are wanting to express the exquisite Delight it afforded to the admiring crouded Audience. The Sublime, the Grand, and the Tender, adapted to the most elevated, majestick and moving Words, conspired to transport and charm the ravished Heart and Ear ...'

RETURN TO LONDON

Handel repeated *Messiah* on June 3, to round off a triumphal season, and then in August 1742 returned to an apparently indifferent London, with the promise ringing in Dublin ears that he would return there next year. He did not, of course, but found himself enmeshed once more in the turmoil of his busy life in the English capital. He completed the one or two odd numbers still wanting in *Samson,* and finally produced the work at Covent Garden in February 1743. He then tentatively put forward *Messiah,* not under its correct title, for fear of offending English puritan susceptibilities, but simply as 'a new sacred oratorio'. It seems to have received little or no attention at the time and Handel appears to have reluctantly decided against it for the time being, much as he had that other great choral masterpiece, *Israel in Egypt.*

HANDEL AND THE ORATORIO

This is perhaps a good place to pause and consider Handel as a composer of oratorios. In general he followed an Italian rather than a German tradition. His roots in that direction go back to Carissimi rather than to Schütz. His first oratorios were Italian, and later on, in England, he had no English models to follow, since no one had preceded him. In any case his earliest English work in the field was not called an oratorio at first, but was known as the 'masque' of *Haman and Mordecai*—only later did this become the 'oratorio' of *Esther*. Even this early work placed considerable emphasis on the chorus, equally as on the soloists. It is here that he differs so much from his Italian models, who placed much more importance on the soloists than on the chorus. England, though, was a land of choral singers, even in Handel's day, and it was not difficult for him to raise a sufficient chorus from the London church choirs. Thus the Handelian type of oratorio developed, evolving partly from his Italian operas, and partly from English dramatic tradition, and in particular the kind of 'study-tragedy' exemplified by Milton's *Samson Agonistes* as well as epics such as *Paradise Lost*. The Handelian oratorio reached its peak in *Messiah* and *Israel in Egypt,* neither of which are particularly characteristic of Handelian oratorio as a whole. The truly typical Handel oratorio is a direct dramatic narrative, told in terms of recitative and aria, with the chorus commenting on the action or describing events, or even 'imitating nature' (that alternative ideal or bugbear of eighteenth century musical criticism). Handel was rather good at using his chorus to depict natural phenomena, and was often castigated by purist critics for doing so.

Handel had his imitators in the oratorio field, but none of the numerous oratorios composed by his English rivals had much success, except perhaps Samuel Arnold, with his *Prodigal son,* and even that has disappeared virtually without trace. The next great oratorios were those of Haydn (*The Creation* and *The Seasons*) avowedly written in imitation of Handel, and then those of Spohr and Mendelssohn—the latter's *Elijah* (1846) remaining the only oratorio which can really match *Messiah* in popularity. (The Bach Passions belong to a completely different line of development, and the so-called *Christmas Oratorio* is not really an oratorio at all, but a mere string of church cantatas which should never be performed *in toto*.)

In many ways Handel still remains the master of the oratorio field, the greatest composer of oratorios who has ever lived, and those works which George Bernard Shaw called 'the great Handelian epics' still remain unrivalled in their own special way. True, we tend to produce them on the stage nowadays, rather as if they were operas; in this new guise some of them work, others certainly do not, chiefly because the music is so big that it gets in the way of the drama, especially where the choruses are concerned. The experiment is always worth making, for in many ways Handelian oratorio is far more dramatic than Handelian opera, which has been described, and not without justification, as 'a concert in costume'. This Handelian oratorio never is, even paradoxically, when it is produced in concert versions. There are few pleasures greater than that of sitting down, score in hand, to listen to a recorded or broadcast performance of a Handel oratorio. Given Handel's superb genius, and a good performance, the mind will provide the *mis-en-scène*.

A NEW PATTERN OF WORK

The summer of 1743 saw him busy with the composition of two new English works, *Semele,* a 'secular oratorio' (to a text originally written by Congreve as an opera libretto) and *Joseph and his brethren.* He also composed a magnificent *Te Deum* for the victory of King George II and his forces at Dettingen—the last battle at which an English king actually commanded an army in the field. *Semele* was first produced at Covent Garden in February 1744 and *Joseph and his brethren* in March. The pattern of life for his later years was now beginning to form, with the composition of two new oratorios each late summer, and their production early in the following year. *Hercules,* another 'secular oratorio' and *Belshazzar,* a biblical one, followed the last pair, *Hercules* being produced at the King's Theatre on January 5 and *Belshazzar* on March 27. Neither were very successful. Factions had been set up against him once again; fashionable people seemed to delight in arranging their grand parties and entertainments on the very nights he was going to give his concerts.

Ill once more, and again in grave financial difficulties, he had to give up his concerts, and was excusably bitter when the rising young opera composer Christopher Willibald Gluck called on him to discuss the subject of British musical taste. That was in the fateful summer of 1745, when Bonnie Prince Charlie and his Jacobite followers reached as far south as Derby before turning back on their tragic and weary homeward retreat to the Highlands, to be eventually cut to pieces on Culloden Moor in April 1746 by 'Butcher Cumberland'. Handel, always a loyal Hanoverian, celebrated the dynastic victory with his *Occasional oratorio,* produced at Covent Garden in the February of 1746, but even so, his usual Lenten oratorio session there was not particularly successful.

However the tide, so long held back, was about to turn. He had found a new librettist in Dr Thomas Morell, a learned parson who could write verses which, if not exactly inspired, were at least competent and apt for musical setting. According to Morell's own memoirs, it was Handel himself who asked Morell to write an oratorio text for him, on the recommendation of the Prince of Wales. Out of this collaboration came one of Handel's most popular oratorios, *Judas Maccabaeus,* appearing at Covent Garden in early April, 1747. Suddenly Handel had acquired a new public. The rich London Jews flocked to hear him sound the praises of their national hero. Handel and Morell, who had been celebrating by proxy the victorious Cumberland, must have been as surprised as anyone when the Jews began flocking to the theatre. Handel, always ready to exploit any show of interest, soon had Morell busy on two new, though similar subjects: *Joshua* and *Alexander Balus.* These he produced at Covent Garden the following Lent. The next pair of oratorios, *Susanna* and *Solomon,* were written between June and August 1748, and produced during Lent, 1749.

THE ROYAL FIREWORKS MUSIC: THE FOUNDLING HOSPITAL
That Lent also saw Handel busy composing one of his most popular instrumental pieces, the *Musick for the Royal Fireworks,* intended for performance during the fireworks display organised to celebrate the Peace of Aix-la-Chapelle, signed the previous year. There was, though, some difficulty over the music. The King, who saw himself as a military man, insisted on 'warlike instruments' only—that is to say, wind instruments, such as oboes and bassoons, trumpets, horns and drums. Handel obviously mistrusted the intonation of such instruments when played without accompaniment, and was

very slow in making up his mind about the score, which he seems to have delayed greatly, finally scribbling it down in his usual impetuous way at the last second. Whether it really was played on the occasion solely by wind instruments, only we shall probably never know—I have a shrewd suspicion myself that Handel had a string band hidden away where the King could not see it. A public rehearsal of the music, at Vauxhall Gardens, was immensely successful and caused one of London's earliest and most notorious traffic-jams. The display itself, held in the Green Park on April 27, 1749, was something of a fiasco, as part of the fireworks ' machine ' caught fire and was destroyed during the performance. Signor Servadoni, its designer, was so mortified that he drew his sword on the poor Comptroller of the Ordnance, whose part in the affair had brought him nothing but trouble. To cap everything, the English April weather displayed its usual fickleness and the day ended with a steady drizzle. But Handel's *Fireworks Music,* thanks to its superb orchestration and wonderful tunes, was launched on its apparently ageless career, and is, if anything, enjoyed more now than ever before.

That same year also saw the beginning of the future popularity of *Messiah,* through Handel's charitable concern with the Foundling Hospital, founded by Captain Thomas Coram in 1740. The ever warm-hearted and generous Handel interested himself deeply in this particular charity, and in the spring of 1749 he offered to organise a benefit concert in the Hospital's newly finished chapel. It was this that led to his annual performances there of *Messiah* which, from the first given in Lent, 1750, were immensely successful.

His next oratorio, *Theodora,* composed in July 1749 and produced in March 1750, was not a great success. Handel, with his usual dry humour, summed up the situation with the observation 'As it is a Christian story, the Jews will not come, and as it is a virtuous story, the ladies will not come, either '. Perhaps it was because of this lack of success that it became one of his own favourites, but how could anyone expect a popular success in an oratorio consisting largely of slow movements? He composed incidental music for an abortive stage piece, *Alceste,* by his friend Tobias Smollett, and after it failed to attain production, used up the music in a charming English serenata, *The Choice of Hercules,* produced in March 1751.

In the summer of 1751, during the composition of his last oratorio, *Jephtha,* he began to experience difficulties with his eyes and had to postpone the completion of that score several times, because of what he called the 'relaxation' of sight in his left eye. He managed to finish the score with great difficulty, and produced it at Covent Garden in late February 1752, during the oratorio season which he held regularly and generally with fair success. The money now began to come in quite steadily, but the great composer found it harder to enjoy life as his sight failed more and more. He faced the horrors of eighteenth century ophthalmic surgery stoically enough, but to little avail. His eyesight was restored for a short period after one operation and high hopes were raised that it had returned permanently. Then glaucoma set in and his sight grew even worse, until he became virtually blind. It became quite fashionable to attend his oratorios and 'enjoy the luxury of tears' as he was led by a boy to the organ, and later brought forward at the end to 'make his customary obeisance' in response to the final applause. At the first onset of blindness he had been despondent and listless, but as it became obvious that he must resign himself to darkness, the old fighting spirit rose in him and he was soon directing his oratorios and playing his organ concertos once more. Mr Sharp, his eye-surgeon, rather tactlessly suggested that it might be a good idea to seek the assistance of John Stanley, the famous blind organist. Handel, who was never one to suffer fools gladly, burst out with 'Oh Mr Sharp, have you not read in the Scripture that if the blind lead the blind they shall both fall into the ditch?'.

Thus his last golden decade, an Indian summer of financial success, gradually drew him towards his inevitable end, as 'the great and good Mr Handel'. Some years saw his concerts crowded, some saw them comparatively empty. Then, as now, *Messiah* would always draw a full house, whilst *Theodora* or *Israel in Egypt* played to empty houses. On one such occasion two of his professional acquaintances requested free tickets for *Messiah*: 'Oh, you are tamnaple tainty, mein Herren!' he is reputed to have cried. ' You would not come to *Teodora*. Dere was room enough to tance dere, when dat was perform '. He was also philosophical enough, in those later days, to console his performers for any empty house by saying ' Neffer moind; de music vill sound de petter!' On the whole, however, those later years were successful enough for him to accumulate some £20,000—a comparatively large sum in those days, when so many musicians died in penury.

In somewhat declining health—he was seventy four years old by now—Handel was still directing and performing during that last memorable season at Covent Garden in 1759 when he became suddenly ill and was forced to retire to bed. There is a final touching report about him, from James Smyth to their mutual friend Bernard Granville:

' London, April 17th, 1759

Dear Sir,

According to your request to me when you left London, that I would let you know when our good friend departed this life, *on Saturday last at 8 o'clock in the morn died the great and good Mr Handel*. He was sensible to the last moment; made a codicil to his will on Tuesday, ordered to be buried privately in Westminster Abbey, and a monument not to exceed £600 for him. I had the pleasure to reconcile him to his old friends; he saw them and forgave them, and let all their legacies stand! In the codicil he left many legacies to his friends, and among the rest he left me £500, and has left to you the two pictures *you formerly gave him*. He took leave of all his friends on Friday morning, and desired to see nobody but the Doctor and Apothecary and myself. At 7 o'clock in the evening he took leave of me, and told me we ' should meet again '; as soon as I was gone he told his servant ' *not* to let me come to him any more, for that he had *now done with the world* '. He died as he lived—a good *Christian*, with a true sense of his duty to God and man, and in perfect charity with all the world. . .

I am, dear sir, You most obedient humble servant,

James Smyth

He has left the Messiah to the Foundling Hospital, and one

thousand pounds to the decayed musicians and their children, and the residue of his fortune to his niece and relations in Germany. He has died worth £20,000, and left legacies with his charities to nearly £6,000. He has got by his Oratorios this year £1,952 2s 8d.'

He died on Saturday, April 14, 1759 (the day after Good Friday) at the age of 74, at peace with the world and secure in his simple, untroubled faith that he was going to meet his God and Saviour, in that Heaven which he had seen in ecstatic vision when he had composed his unsurpassed Hallelujah chorus. He had asked that he might be privately buried in the Abbey, but it was a request made in vain. Being so celebrated it was inevitable that he should be given a public funeral.

He did get one last wish though. He had requested that a monument should be erected to his memory, and so the famous French sculptor, Roubiliac, was commissioned to carve another famous Handel statue, to follow the earlier one which Handel's old friend Jonathan Tyers had commissioned for Vauxhall, and which is still to be seen in the Victoria and Albert Museum.

HANDEL'S CHARACTER AND GENIUS

In many ways, Handel is still an enigma. The world knows and loves his music, probably now as never before, but the man himself escapes us still, hidden behind the almost Johnsonesque figure of the anecdotes. That he was a very big man, with a very brusque temper but a very generous heart, all the world knows, as it knows that he never entirely mastered spoken English, although he could write it adequately. Even so, he left few letters, and those which have survived are mostly rather stiff and formal, and reveal all too little of his inward thoughts. Of his private life we know practically nothing—what he read (apart from the Bible), and what he really believed apart from the accepted truths of Holy Writ. He had a number of women friends, but we know practically nothing of his relations with them, except that they seem to have been platonic. Burney says that 'Handel's amours were brief and confined to persons of his own profession', a statement which merely whets

41

curiosity without in the least satisfying it. There is certainly not the slightest breath of scandal connected with Handel's private life. The one slightly amoral inclination which can be charged against him is his lifelong habit of borrowing other people's tunes. In this it is best perhaps to be patient and remember again Dr Boyce's injunction that Handel 'took other men's pebbles and polished them into diamonds'. That he was no pious, stuffed wax lay figure is evident; he was a very vital, warm-hearted man who could be thrown into a passion one minute, only to be profuse with apology the next, if he found he was in the wrong. In many ways he was a hedonistic old pagan; time and again in his oratorios one has the feeling that his sympathies lay, not with the pious and often boring Children of Israel, but with the healthy, down to earth, warm blooded pagans who were their opponents. And he wrote some of the most exquisite love-music in existence for certain of his female characters. Truly, a very complex person, of whose inner life we still know too little—it may be that we shall never know much more. Yet he set his mark on eighteenth century England as truly as did Dr Johnson himself, with whom in fact he has a great deal in common.

As a composer Handel's reputation has always stood very high. His immense gifts were recognised even in his youth, and to his English contemporaries he was not merely a great composer, but the greatest one who had ever lived. That reputation outlasted his mortal span, and his music continued to be held in the highest regard, in a century when music-lovers generally preferred the very latest music to anything that had been written perhaps only a few years previously. His two great contemporaries, J S Bach and Georg Philipp Telemann, both suffered a period of posthumous neglect which never befell Handel.

What contributed to this great reputation? Certainly not originality, in the modern sense, for Handel was no seeker after originality, as such. True he achieved many strikingly original effects, but it was usually by the use of traditional methods. In music certainly, he was more a conservative than a radical and in general his style broadened, rather than developed, as his life wore on, so much so that it is often very difficult to tell if a piece by him dates from the beginning or end of his musical career. His English contemporaries referred to his rather grand manner as 'the open and manly style of Handel'. There was indeed a combination of grandeur and simplicity in his music which appealed very much to his Georgian contemporaries. If his music is sometimes almost too leisurely and prolix for modern audiences, this is more than compensated for by his wonderful fluent melody, as well as his profound understanding of human emotions and his gift for expressing them in music.

As a master of counterpoint and fugue he was hardly surpassed even by the great Johann Sebastian himself; he could achieve great choral effects by means so simple that they are still the despair of more subtle and sophisticated minds. As an orchestrator, too, his methods were simple, but sure. He seems to have known by instinct exactly the effect he wanted and how to get it by the most direct means. One has only to think of the score of the *Musick for the Royal Fireworks,* or the magnificent *Concerti a due cori,* to realise this. He was, naturally, a superb keyboard player, particularly at the organ, so that as the years drew on the performance of his own organ concertos became a leading feature of his oratorios. In those concertos there was always a strong tendency towards free improvisation, and it has been said, not without some truth, that in a way, all Handel's music is magnificent improvisation—improvisation which he happened to write down, instead of merely providing on the spot. He did, of course, usually compose at lightning speed. There is, in truth, not a little of Shakespearean largeness about his music. In the final judgment, one places him firmly among the truly great ones, that handful of immortals which includes Shakespeare and Michelangelo and Beethoven and Goethe, and he is by no means the least among them.

Books in English about Handel

Handel's work and personality made a deep impression on his age, and that impression has continued ever since, leading to a great many books and articles being written about him, his personality, works and times. Over the years, there have also been a number of Handel societies devoted to the publication, propagation and performance of his works. An annual volume, the *Händel-Jahrbuch*, has been published by the present German Handel Society since 1955, dealing with all matters of interest to Handelians, and giving information concerning new publications about him, his life and works. In this context, mention should also be made of Konrad Sasse's *Händel-Bibliographie* (Deutscher Verlag für Musik, Leipzig, 1963), a comprehensive classified list of all books, articles and reviews published before 1962. (A supplement covering the years 1962-1965 appeared in 1967.) It is indispensable for the study of Handel, and includes a fairly high proportion of entries for English material.

DOCUMENTS AND LETTERS

The one great volume with which all contemporary Handel study must begin with is Otto Erich Deutsch's massive *Handel: a documentary biography* (Black, 1955). In this magnificent book Deutsch brought together all the then known documents of Handel's life, combining them skilfully into one vivid chronological narration, far more compelling and dramatic than any ordinary biography could hope to be. The medium of documentary biography, as applied to musical subjects, was Deutsch's own special invention. He had practised it at home in Vienna, on the subject of Schubert, long before he came to England as a refugee from Hitler's invasion of Austria. Its most triumphant expression, though, was his splendid Handelian 'documentary' which he dedicated quite simply 'to England, his second Fatherland', leaving us to guess whether it was Handel's fatherland or Deutsch's own which was implied. There are errors and omissions in the book, of course—what else can one expect in a wide-ranging volume running to nearly a thousand pages? Considering its bulk, the errors in it are remarkably few and it can be regarded not merely as a biography but as something of a bibliography as well, containing a great deal of information concerning the publication as well as the early performances of Handel's works. The actual 'Bibliography' section, printed at the end of the volume, is extensive to say the least.

Pre-dating 'Deutsch', but still very useful, is E H Müller's *The letters and writings of G F Handel* (Cassell, 1935). The actual documents it contains are all reprinted in Deutsch of course, but it is still very useful to have them brought together in one small volume. Since 1955, however, a number of other letters relative to Handel have been discovered and new editions of either Deutsch or Müller would have to include these.

BIOGRAPHIES—EIGHTEENTH AND NINETEENTH CENTURIES
Soon after Handel's death in 1759, the Reverend John Mainwaring, Rector of Church Stretton in Shropshire, wrote *Memoirs of the life of the late George Frederic Handel, to which is added a catalogue of his works and observations upon them,* which he published anonymously (Dodsley, 1760, reprinted Knuf, Amsterdam, 1964). This was not only the first complete biography of Handel, but also the first on any one composer in the English language. Many later biographies, including Deutsch's great work, are much indebted to Mainwaring's pioneer effort which drew on many valuable contemporary sources, including the recollections of the Smiths, father and son. Later in the eighteenth century another very important sourcebook published was Dr Charles Burney's *An account of the musical performances in Westminster Abbey* (Payne & Robinson,

45

1785, reprinted Knuf, Amsterdam, 1964). This account of the first major Handel festival, which took place in the Abbey in 1784, includes not only copious programme notes on the concerts themselves with lists of performers, but also a useful ' Sketch of the life of Handel ', as well as many entertaining and illuminating anecdotes about the composer, many of which are not included in Deutsch. Another fascinating early source is the anonymous *Anecdotes of George Frideric Handel and John Christopher Smith* (Cadell & Davies, 1799). Its author was long considered to be the Reverend William Coxe, but modern scholarship is doubtful of this attribution. John Christopher Smith was the son of Handel's amanuensis Johann Christopher Smith and was himself Handel's assistant at the harpsichord in the performances of his later works. The book is to some extent more about him than about Handel, but it still contains a certain amount of important information about the great composer. A reprint has been announced, but has not as yet appeared.

A short while before Queen Victoria came to the throne, a curious publication appeared under the title of *Reminiscences of Handel, His Grace the Duke of Chandos, Powells the harpers, the Harmonious Blacksmith, and others* . . . (privately printed, 1836)— I quote only part of its very long-winded title! This odd book was written and published by one Richard Clark, a Gentleman of the Chapel Royal. Although serious in intent, its theories concerning the origin of the *Harmonious Blacksmith* variations cannot be taken very seriously at all—Clark even produced an engraving of the legendary Blacksmith's even more mythical anvil—and indeed the whole book is nowadays regarded as something of a joke. Clark also wrote a book *On the sacred oratorio of the Messiah* (privately printed, 1852), but he was at best only a skirmisher in the Handelian field, and a rather untrustworthy one at that.

During Clark's lifetime other and more trustworthy Handelians were at work. Amongst them was the great German Handelian Friedrich Chrysander (1826-1901) who besides his long labours as sole editor of the magnificent series of Händel-Gesellschaft volumes, wrote a biography (in German) of his hero which, although incomplete and never translated into English, has still put all subsequent

46

biographers into his debt. Chrysander had a French contemporary, Victor Schoelcher (1804-1893), who wrote the excellent *Life of Handel*, which was translated into English by James Lowe (Cocks, 1857). It is still of special interest, not merely because of its high intrinsic value—Schoelcher was a man of considerable scholarship and much application—but also simply because it was by a Frenchman, a member of a race who as a general rule were not the most ardent admirers of Handel's music. (One remembers Schoelcher's brilliant compatriot Berlioz dismissing Handel contemptuously as ' a barrel of pork and beer '—a somewhat ill-founded sneer, as we do not know if Handel was especially fond of pork and in any case his favourite tipple seems to have been wine, not beer.) One would not really expect the great Frenchman to understand the even mightier Saxon; they saw music from somewhat extreme angles although both startled the ears of their contemporaries, if only with the noisiness of their performances. But to return to Schoelcher: he lived for many years in England as a political refugee, and there fell in love with Handel's music. He formed a very fine collection of Handeliana, which he took back to Paris with him on his eventual return, and which is now in the care of the music department at the Bibliothèque Nationale in Paris.

A Victorian biography which is often either overlooked or merely mentioned with condescension, though still very much worth reading, is W S Rockstro's *Life of G F Handel* (Macmillan, 1883). Rockstro, who was a notable historian and teacher of counterpoint, knew Handelian sources very well, and was one of the first to urge a return to the composer's original intentions with regard to instrumentation, instead of the monstrous travesties of it which were still the rule in Victorian performances. Among Rockstro's pupils was that redoubtable ' Handelator ' Samuel Butler, whose writings are full of references to Handel and his works and who composed, in collaboration with his friend H Festing Jones, a couple of mock-Handelian comic oratorios. It was Butler who put forward the theory, somewhat shocking to his Victorian contemporaries, that one can be in love with your hero and still laugh at him, as Butler was (and did) with Handel.

47

Towards the turn of the century we come to a spate of Handelian biographies and studies. In 1893 the *Musical times* published a Handel supplement which is still valuable. It contains much interesting biographical and historical information, contributed by W H Cummings, A H Mann and others, not easy to find elsewhere, even in Deutsch. Then in 1901, that distinguished academician C F Abdy Williams produced *Handel, his life and works*, for the ' Master Musicians series ' (Dent, 1901). This was a work very typical of its conscientious author, more celebrated perhaps nowadays for his still extremely useful work on university degrees in music. Abdy Williams's biography of Handel was reprinted as late as 1935, in a revision by Eric Blom. In 1906 the perspicacious Cambridge scholar Sedley Taylor produced a shrewd study *The indebtedness of Handel to other composers* (Cambridge University Press, 1906) which was among the first to bring the problem of Handel's borrowings out into the full light of critical day. Chrysander, it is true, had published several of the sources, in the supplementary volumes to his Händel-Gesellschaft edition. Boyce had excused Handel's borrowings, while Crotch had more than suspected them. It was left, nevertheless, to Sedley Taylor to bring the problem of these plagiarisms clearly before the British public. Shocked and outraged, Percy Robinson produced a sharp rejoinder in *Handel and his orbit* (Sherratt & Hughes, Manchester, 1908) in which the author tried to prove that Handel was not really a plagiarist at all and that Erba and Urio, two of the composers whom Sedley Taylor had laid heavily under contribution, were not really composers at all, but merely places in Italy where Handel stayed. The evidence, however, has proved to be completely against Robinson, and since 1908 many new facts have accumulated which have all tended to prove that Taylor was right and Robinson was wrong. There seems little doubt now that, as explained on page 30, Handel was a plagiarist of the first order, and most later writers have been more concerned with excusing than denying his musical misdemeanours. Nonetheless, the theories which Robinson tried so hard to establish must still be given some consideration, even by those who dismiss his conclusions.

The year after Robinson's somewhat mistaken book appeared, one of the great classics of Handelian literature was published. This was R A Streatfeild's *Handel* (The New Library of Music, 1907; 2nd ed Methuen, 1909, reprinted with revisions by J Merrill Knapp, Da Capo, NY, 1960). Streatfeild, another friend of Samuel Butler and much influenced by him, was a most careful and conscientious scholar, who sought, as he says in his preface, ' to elucidate the inner meaning of Handel's music, and its power of searching the profoundest recesses of the soul '. Streatfeild wrote several books on musical subjects, including two others on Handel (see also page 58). He followed up his Handel biography with a much smaller though still important work on *Handel, Canons and the Duke of Chandos* (Chiswick Press, 1916) which threw some much needed light on Handel's service with the ' Princely Chandos '. That same year also saw the appearance of Romain Rolland's *Handel,* first published in the French in 1910 and translated into English by A Eaglefield Hull (Kegan Paul, 1916). This work is still of great interest, not merely because it came from the pen of a great French man of letters but also because of his typically Gallic view that Handel's oratorio overtures had programmatic significance. Rolland was also one of the first to urge the stage revival of Handel's operas. At the close of World War I an interesting topographical miniature appeared in the guise of J C Sibley's *Handel at Canons: with a description of the church of St Lawrence, Whitchurch* (Musical Exchange, 1918) which added its mite to the bulkier previous works on the subject.

Some five years later one of the most celebrated, although not one of the best, Handel biographies appeared. This was Sir Newman Flower's *George Frideric Handel, his personality and times* (Cassell, 1923; last revised edition, 1959). Flower's volume was for many years the most widely-read English book on Handel. Its author was an enthusiastic collector of Handeliana (including the voluminous ' Smith ' transcripts now in the Henry Watson Library, Manchester) and his celebrated book is highly personal and idiosyncratic, though disfigured by an odd mixture of priggishness and sentimentality. Despite this it should still be read by even the serious student of Handel's life. There is, curiously enough, very little about

49

Handel's music in Flower's bulky volume. Perhaps its chief merit is in the bibliography, compiled by William C Smith, a veteran Handelian whose name so frequently appears in these pages.

Some years elapsed before another notable Handel biography appeared in English and even then it was a slender volume, but a miniature masterpiece by the greatest of all English musical scholars, E J Dent. His little book *Handel* (Duckworth, 1934 'Great Lives' series) displays all Dent's usual clarity of thought and expression and is quite indispensable. It also offers some interesting contributions to our understanding of Handel's plagiarisms. No major biographies of Handel appeared in English for some time after Dent's book, the wartime market being held by Newman Flower and Blom's revision of Abdy Williams in the 'Master Musicians' series. One little-known work did appear in 1946. This was Hubert Weinstock's *Handel* (Knopf, NY) which was dismissed by Alfred Mann and J Merrill Knapp (in their authoritative article 'The present state of Handel research' in *Acta musicologica,* vol. XLI, fasc 1-2, Bärenreiter, Basle, 1969) as being written 'somewhat in the style of Emil Ludwig's historical novels'. The next year though, saw publication of an important new biography. Abdy Williams' volume in the 'Master Musicians series' had been out for nearly fifty years when it was replaced by Percy M Young's *Handel* (Dent, 1947, last reprinted 1968), which proved to be one of this prolific author's best books. It is an admirable work, concise and packed with fresh ideas including some new information about Handel's general finances.

After a rather dull interlude, several new biographies appeared in the sixties. The noted Handelian Dr James S Hall, President of the Deal and Walmer Handel Society, wrote an illuminating monograph, *G F Handel,* issued in the 'Great Masters' series by Boosey & Hawkes (1961, revised and enlarged edition, 1963). The early sixties also saw the appearance of one or two so profusely illustrated that they are almost in the picture-book class. One such work, of Germanic origins but issued over here in an English translation, is Werner Rackwitz and Helmut Stefan's *George Frideric Handel: a biography in pictures* (VEB Editions, Leipzig, 1962). Its illustrations are excellent, and its text is also most informative. The same is equally true of Stanley Sadie's stimulating *Handel* (Calder, 1962). The same author's book for young people, *Handel* (Faber, 1968) may be warmly recommended: it includes well chosen excerpts from the music, arranged for piano.

The latest, and undoubtedly one of the most extensive of all Handel biographies in English is Paul Henry Lang's *George Frideric Handel* (Norton, NY, 1966; Faber, 1966). In this massive labour of love, the distinguished author of *Music in western civilisation* applies all his extensive knowledge of the social and intellectual background of eighteenth century society to the subject of Handel. Lang's book was controversial, although less so to English than to American readers. To British Handelians his views seem less startingly original, since so many of his apparently daring premises have long been accepted here. He certainly did great good in clearing away many old misconceptions and his crusade against the Teutonic myth that Handel was above all a German composer and not a great eclectic, was well worth attempting, particularly in his own country where musicology has long tended to follow Germanic precedent. From the point of view of this present chapter, one of the most interesting sections of Lang's whole massive tome is his own chapter XXVII, devoted to Handelian biography and comparative studies, in which he deals out some blows at a number of his predecessors in the field.

There are several books of collected papers and studies which are of considerable importance for Handel studies. Foremost amongst these is *Handel: a symposium,* edited by Gerald Abraham (OUP, 1954). This indispensable book contains generally authoritative articles by some of the leading British Handel scholars of the age: Percy Young on ' Handel the man '; E J Dent on ' The operas '; Julian Herbage on ' The oratorios and cantatas '; Basil Lam on ' The church music '; and ' The orchestral music '; Anthony Lewis on ' The songs and chamber cantatas '; Kathleen Dale on ' The keyboard music '; John Horton on ' The chamber music '; Gerald Abraham himself discussing ' Some points of style ', and lastly William C Smith rounds off the volume with a quite invaluable catalogue of works, which, as the author himself states, was planned in quite a different manner from his companion catalogue appended to the Handel article in the fifth edition of Grove's *Dictionary of music and musicians* (Macmillan, 1954).

From the 1920s onwards, William C Smith established for himself a considerable reputation as a Handel scholar with various articles of great bibliographical or historical importance, of which a selection was reprinted in his *Concerning Handel: his life and works* (Cassell, 1948). These essays include: 'Handel the man'; 'Finance and patronage in Handel's life'; 'The earliest editions of Messiah'; 'Some Handel portraits reconsidered'; 'Handel's failure in 1747'; 'New letters of the composer'; 'Gustavus Waltz: was he Handel's cook?'; '*Acis and Galatea* in the eighteenth century'; 'The earliest editions of the *Water Music*', and they were preceded by a foreword by Sir Newman Flower. Some seventeen years later Smith followed this volume with an autobiographical work, *A Handelian's notebook* (Black, 1965) which, although it tells us perhaps rather more about Smith than it does about Handel, is nevertheless full of information about Handelian sources, performances, bibliography, and the like. It also contains in an appendix a list of the author's own writings on musical subjects, including many items 'concerning Handel'.

As a pendant to biographies, we should not overlook *Handel at Vauxhall* (Victoria and Albert Museum Bulletin Reprints, 1, 1969), a well illustrated booklet by Terence Hodgkinson, which describes Roubiliac's famous statue, its situation in Vauxhall Gardens, its subsequent history and acquisition by the Museum. Finally, there is —for exceptional mention, an unique essay which, though not strictly biographical can best be cited here. It provided the title for a book by H G Farmer, *Handel's kettledrums and other papers on military music* (Hinrichsen, 1950). This essay describes the huge drums which Handel borrowed from the Tower of London for some specific performances. Farmer also includes some fascinating contemporary documents.

GENERAL CRITICISM

Let us now turn to studies of certain aspects of Handel and his music. It is curious that although the idea of comparing Handel with his great compatriot and contemporary J S Bach is one which often seems uppermost in the minds of examiners for degrees in music, few scholars have actually devoted much time to it. The notable exception to this is Archibald T Davison, whose *Bach and Handel, the consummation of the Baroque in music* (Harvard University Press, Cambridge, Mass, 1951) is the one full-scale study of the subject in English. Handel's own methods of composition are examined in great detail in John Tobin's *Handel at work* (Cassell, 1964).

THE ORATORIOS

The oratorios have been the subject of various studies. Percy M Young's *The oratorios of Handel* (Dobson, 1948) was a good general survey, but has been eclipsed by one of the greatest of all Handelian classics, Winton Dean's magnificent *Handel's dramatic oratorios and masques* (OUP, 1959), an exhaustive work which overshadows all previous efforts in this particular field. It blends critical insight with impeccable scholarship, and its author handles with the utmost ease all the minutiae of cast-lists, not only for the first performances of the oratorios but for the revivals which took place during Handel's lifetime. Much more specialised is Robert Manson Myers' *Early moral criticism of Handelian oratorio* (Manson Park Press, Williamsburg, 1947), which is important for showing the extraordinary way in which the human mind can react adversely to what later generations regard as the most innocent causes. The same author's *Handel, Dryden and Milton* (Bowes & Bowes, 1956) is of equal interest for the literary background of Handelian oratorio.

MESSIAH

Turning from the broad general aspect of Handelian oratorio, we approach *the* Handel oratorio—*Messiah,* which has naturally provoked a number of studies over the years. One little-known though extremely interesting Victorian work on the subject is James C Culwick's *Handel's Messiah: discovery of the original word-book used at the first performance in Dublin, April 13, 1742; with some notes* (Ponsonby & Weldrick, 1891). A quarter of a century or so later came J Allanson Benson's *Handel's Messiah, the oratorio and its history* (Reeves, 1923), an attempt to present in handbook form various useful hints as to the practical performance. Another work of the same decade was E C Bairstow's *Handel's oratorio the Messiah* (OUP, 1928), one of the ' Musical Pilgrim ' series, and still well worth reading. Published some twenty years later, Julian Herbage's *The Messiah* in ' The world of music ' series (Parrish, 1948) gives a fascinating literary and pictorial account of the work, linked with some notable broadcast performances of the author's pioneering version of the score ' as it was writ '. R M Myers reappears here with his *Handel's Messiah: a touchstone of taste* (NY, Macmillan, 1948) which again stresses the literary, rather than the musical, background.

The present time has been remarkable for some very close studies of the actual manuscript sources and the copyists who were responsible for the original *Messiah* material as it has come down to us over the years. The eminent Danish scholar Jens Peter Larsen has given us, in *Handel's Messiah: origins, composition, sources* (Black, 1957), an authoritative study which examines not only the various early performances of *Messiah* given by Handel, but also investigates the phenomenon of the numerous copyists usually hidden under the general patronymic ' Smith '—' the factory ' as some scholars have described them. Larsen has identified thirteen copyists in the ' Smith ' circle, and over thirty others who probably worked outside it. His book is therefore quite indispensable for anyone who is called upon to deal with the early manuscript copies of Handel's works. Some of them assume prime importance when the actual autograph is missing, as in the case of the *Water Music*. Larsen lists the manuscript sources for ninety one works or groups.

Harold Watkins Shaw is another outstanding modern scholar who has devoted much time and energy to investigating the textual problems concerning *Messiah*. His two studies *The story of Handel's Messiah, 1741-1784. A short popular history* (Novello, 1963) and *A textual and historical companion to Handel's Messiah* (Novello, 1965), parallel to some extent Larsen's work, but are quite independent of the latter's achievement and show this English scholar's deep knowledge of the various sources. (His editions are listed on pages 73, 74 and 79). Another English researcher who has concerned himself greatly with *Messiah,* both theoretically and practically (by his notable performances) is John Tobin, whose *Handel at work* has already been referred to, and whose *Handel's Messiah: a critical account of the manuscript sources and printed editions* (Cassell, 1969) gives much useful information concerning such source materials although it has been criticised for not being as exhaustive as it might be. One of its chief interests is that it reprints many of the additional vocal ornaments used by the author in his own *Messiah* performances from 1950 onwards.

THE OPERAS

Curiously enough there have been very few works in English dealing wholly with Handel's operas. For a great many years one of the very few English attempts to deal with them was E J Dent's rather superficial chapter in the *Handel symposium* mentioned above (page 51). Recently, however, the series of Ernest Bloch Lectures delivered by Winton Dean at the University of California in 1965/66, have been published under the title of *Handel and the opera seria* (OUP, 1970). Dean writes most perceptively about Handel's theatrical craftsmanship, and categorises several distinct types of opera. He is also critical of what he considers musical malpractices in modern revivals.

EXHIBITION CATALOGUES

Last of all we come to exhibition catalogues, a type of literature which often adds significantly to our store of information about the sources of a composer's music and the background of his life, as they enshrine facts which are valuable long after the occasion of the exhibition has passed. Without diving too much into the past, we may mention the record of an important exhibition, under the title *Commemorative exhibition of the two hundred and fiftieth anniversary of the births of George Friderick Handel, 1685-1759, and Johann Sebastian Bach, 1685-1750* (Cambridge University Press, 1935). This was held at the Fitzwilliam Museum, and the catalogue forms an instructive complement to Davidson's study of the two composers (page 53). Scotland staged a memorable exhibition which drew on a number of public and private collections, besides its own national resources. The catalogue was entitled: *George Frideric Handel 1685-1759. Catalogue of an exhibition held during the Edin-*

burgh Musical Festival, with an introduction by William C Smith (National Library of Scotland, Edinburgh, 1948).

The fashion for Handel exhibitions was continued three years later with *Handel's Messiah. Catalogue of an exhibition held May-July, 1951* (Trustees of the British Museum, 1951). This brought together most of the primary sources for the works, including the manuscript scores from Hamburg and Tenbury. The bicentenary of Handel's death in 1959 was linked with the probable tercentenary of Purcell's birth, and a joint exhibition was held in the British Museum in connection with the national festival of their music. The catalogue listed the principal autographs, first editions and many illustrations relating to both composers. It was entitled: *Henry Purcell 1659(?)-1695. George Frideric Handel 1685-1759. Catalogue of a commemorative exhibition* (Trustees of the British Museum, 1959). (This, like the *Messiah* catalogue, was the work of A Hyatt King.) Finally we may list an important record of that occasion, which was edited by Nigel Fortune under the title *Purcell-Handel Festival, London, June 1959* (the Festival Committee, 1959). It contained essays on Handel by some notable specialists, including 'Handel in England' by Julian Herbage, 'Handel's dramatic works' by Winton Dean, 'Handel and the English Church' by Basil Lam and 'Handel's musical instruments' by H F Redlich, as well as a short but penetrating comparison of Handel and Purcell, by J A Westrup.

Editions of Handel's Music

Any account of the editions of a composer's works should, one feels, begin with reference to a thematic catalogue, but in Handel's case this is, alas, still impossible. Handel is virtually alone amongst the great composers in having no thematic catalogue of his work published. Friedrich Chrysander planned one as a supplement to his biography of Handel, but unfortunately it never appeared in print. The distinguished American Handel scholar, the late J M Coopersmith, had actually prepared a catalogue in manuscript, but it is reputed to be so unwieldy in its present state that it too is likely to remain unpublished. Various schemes are afoot in America to prepare computerised catalogues of Handel's music, but how far these have progressed towards publication is still a matter of some conjecture. Meanwhile A Craig Bell has published a *Chronological catalogue of Handel's works* (Grain-Aig Press, Greenock, 1969) which, while not a thematic catalogue, is a catalogue raisonée, without musical incipits. It has been criticised for some inaccuracy and inconsistency, but it is nevertheless very useful, and presents a handy scheme of identification which has been employed in the ensuing pages of this chapter, under the symbol CB (*ie* Craig Bell). Smaller, though in many ways a lot more accurate, are the two lists prepared by William C Smith and published in books such as Grove's *Dictionary of music and musicians* (5th ed, 1954) and Gerald Abraham's *Handel: a symposium* (see page 51), and which still represent the most trustworthy guides to Handel's musical output.

57

Of particular value here is the same author's collaboration with his former British Museum colleague Charles Humphries in their joint *Handel: a descriptive catalogue of the early editions* (Cassell, 1960, second edition Blackwell, Oxford 1970), which is quite as indispensable for Handelian bibliography as ' Deutsch ' is for the biography.

A Hyatt King's *Handel and his autographs* (British Museum, 1967) is equally indispensable to any really earnest student of the original manuscript sources: to a large extent it supersedes R A Streatfeild's *Handel autographs at the British Museum* (British Museum, 1912) and greatly supplements W Barclay Squire's ' The Handel Manuscripts ', vol 1 of the *Catalogue of the King's music library* (British Museum, 1927). Barclay Squire's catalogue was printed some forty four years ago—a long time indeed in the history of modern musicology—and there have naturally been a certain number of new discoveries, re-attributions and so on, in the intervening years, but it still stands as one of the most informative lists of Handelian autographs and early copies.

Another catalogue of similar genre is the Handelian section of the *Catalogue of the music in the Fitzwilliam Museum, Cambridge,* edited by J A Fuller-Maitland and A H Mann (Cambridge University Press, 1893). The Fitzwilliam Handel manuscripts were catalogued by Mann, one of the greatest of all English Handelians, and his notes on them are still of immense value to scholars. His equally valuable notes on, and catalogue of, the W Barrett Lennard collection of ' Smith ' copies (acquired by the museum after the publication of the 1893 catalogue) are preserved in the museum library, but have remained unpublished. The Barrett Lennard collection renders the Fitzwilliam Museum's Handel collection doubly useful, especially in those cases in which the autograph is missing. In such cases, the early copies assume a special importance. Another splendid collection of ' Smith ' copies, formerly the property of the late Sir Newman Flower, is now in the Henry Watson Library in Manchester; a provisional list has been prepared by the music librarian, Leonard Duck, and has been circulated in mimeographed copies. Abroad the largest and most important collection of manuscripts comprises the ' Smith ' copies in the State and University Library at Hamburg.

58

Handel is unusual among late Baroque composers in that a great deal of his music was published in his own lifetime, as listed in Smith's descriptive catalogue. True, those editions were often woefully incomplete and very inaccurate (two facts which do not seem to have bothered the composer unduly!) but the music was at least printed and hence widely disseminated throughout Great Britain and the Colonies. The greatest disparities between Handel's original scores and the printed editions of Walsh and his rivals are in the vocal works, where operas and oratorios were printed as mere collections of songs, with scarce a hint of recitatives or choruses. The instrumental works were treated more generously, although even they were printed in parts only, without scores. Handel's immense prestige as a composer eventually led to proposals being made for printing a complete edition of his works, an idea which received considerable impetus from the success of the first great Handel Commemoration, in 1784. Burney seems to have been the original instigator of the proposal, and reprints in his *Account* of the Commemoration (page 45) an advertisement on behalf of Robert Birchall, the music publisher, to publish by subscription ' a uniform and complete edition of Handel's works, to be engraved in score '. Nothing much seems to have come of this idea at first, but in 1786 another notice appeared, this time on behalf of Dr Samuel Arnold with Messrs Longman and Broderip named as agents to collect the subscriptions, together with Birchall. The first of Arnold's 180 numbers appeared in May 1787 and the last in September 1797. The edition, though, was never complete; only four of the Italian operas were included, presumably because Arnold thought the Handelian opera seria was so outmoded that there was little chance of its being revived in his own time, whereas the oratorios were still in considerable demand. Thus his edition was largely devoted to the instrumental music and to the vocal works with English words. Unfortunately Arnold, as an editor, was more enthusiastic than accurate, and his edition is disfigured by many omissions, mistakes and even downright falsifications. Despite this, some of its numbers still have to be consulted in cases where the prime sources are missing. It also has the distinction of being the world's first ' collected edition ' in the field of music.

(*See* J M Coopersmith, ' The first Gesamtausgabe: Dr Arnold's edition of Handel's works ', in *Notes* vol IV, 1946-7; also P Hirsch, ' Dr Arnold's Handel edition (1787-1797),' in *The music review* vol VIII, 1947.)

THE LONDON HANDEL SOCIETY EDITION

The next important development took place in 1843 when the Handel Society of London was formed, with the intention of producing a more accurate complete edition than that of Arnold. Subscriptions were requested ' for the production of a superior and standard edition of the works of Handel ' in full score, and the publishers were Cramer, Addison and Beale. Fourteen volumes were eventually produced, the editors including such distinguished musicians as Mendelssohn, Moscheles, Sterndale Bennett, Sir George Smart, Rimbault and G A Macfarren. The society itself failed through lack of subscribers in 1848, but the publishers continued to issue volumes until 1858. Some of them, particularly *Israel in Egypt* edited by Mendelssohn, are of considerable interest for their prefaces and for his editing of the organ continuo; Mendelssohn refused to add any ' additional accompaniments '.

CHRYSANDER AND THE GERMAN HANDEL SOCIETY'S COMPLETE EDITION

The London Handel Society was succeeded by the German Handel Society (Deutsche Händel Gesellschaft) which began its career in 1856 with the aim of producing ' a critical and uniform edition of the whole of Handel's works in full score, with pianoforte arrangement and German translation of the text'. Its first prospectus was dated August 15, 1856 and among its thirty five signatories was Friedrich Chrysander, through whose editorial enthusiasm and capacity for sheer hard work the edition was at length completed (in 1902). Some uncomplimentary things have been said in recent years about Chrysander's editorial methods, and although he understandably lacked some of the refinements of musical scholarship which have been developed since his death, his monumental edition (usually referred to as ' HG ') is still the only available printed version for many of Handel's works, in particular the operas. Chrysander gave comparatively little information about the sources he used, but that information which he did give is printed in each volume. Between 1929 and 1934, a short supplementary series of music by Handel appeared, edited for practical performance by Max Seiffert and others, and published as ' Veröffentlichungen der Händel-Gesellschaft ' by Breitkopf & Härtel. There appeared in connection with this series the first *Händel-Jahrbuch* which ran from 1928 to 1933 only (see page 44). Vols 1-18 of HG were issued by Breitkopf (1858-64), vols 19-96 by Chrysander himself, at Bergedorf near Hamburg (1864-92), and were followed by six supplementary volumes (page 64). Vol 39 was never published and *Messiah* (vol 45) was published after Chrysander's death, in 1902. The contents of the volumes are as follows :

1 *Susanna* (Oratorio).
2 Keyboard music, collections 1-4.
  Collections 1-2, 16 Suites.
  Collection 3, Miscellaneous pieces.
  Collection 4, 6 fugues.
3 *Acis and Galatea* (Masque).
4 *Hercules* (Oratorio).
5 *Athalia* (Oratorio) .
6 *L'allegro, il penseroso ed il moderato* (Oratorio).
7 *Semele* (Oratorio).
8 *Theodora* (Oratorio).
9 *The Passion according to St John*
10 *Samson* (Oratorio).
11 Funeral anthem for Queen Caroline (*The ways of Zion do mourn*).
12 *Alexander's Feast* (Ode).
13 *Saul* (Oratorio).
14 Coronation anthems (4).
15 *Brockes passion.*
16 *Israel in Egypt* (Oratorio).
17 *Joshua* (Oratorio).

18 *The choice of Hercules* (Musical interlude).
19 *Belshazzar* (Oratorio).
20 *The triumph of time and truth.*
21 Concertos.
  6 Concerti grossi, op 3.
  1 Concerto in *Alexander's Feast.*
  3 Concertos for solo oboe and strings.
  1 Sonata or concerto in B flat for solo violin and strings.
22 *Judas Maccabaeus* (Oratorio).
23 *Ode for St Cecilia's Day.*
24 *Il Tronfo del tempo e della verità* (Oratorio).
25 *Dettingen Te Deum.*
26 *Solomon* (Oratorio).
27 *Sonate da camera.*
  I   15 solo Sonatas.
  II 6 sonatas for 2 oboes and bass.

III 9 sonatas for 2 violins and bass.	28 6 organ concertos, op 4. 6 organ concertos, op 7.
IV 6 sonatas for 2 violins and bass.	29 *Deborah* (Oratorio). 30 12 concerti grossi, op 6.

31 *Te Deum* and *Jubilate* for the Peace of Utrecht.

32 *Duetti and Terzetti*. There were two editions. A full list of titles is given in Grove, 1954, vol IV, pages 54, 55.

33 *Alexander Balus* (Oratorio).

34 Chandos anthems

No 1 *O be joyful;* 2 *In the Lord;* 3 *Have mercy upon me;* 4 *O sing unto the Lord;* 5 *I will magnify Thee;* 6 *As pants the hart.*

35 Chandos anthems

No 7 *My song shall be alway;* 8 *O come let us sing;* 9 *O praise the Lord;* 10 *The Lord is my light;* 11 *Let God arise* (2 versions).

36 Miscellaneous anthems

12 *O praise the Lord, ye angels of his;* 13 Wedding anthem A, *This is the day;* 14 Wedding anthem B, *Sing unto God;* 15 *The King shall rejoice;* 16 Foundling Hospital anthem, *Blessed are they* plus Appendix containing variants of Chandos anthem 4, *O sing unto the Lord* and 6, *As pants the hart.*

37 Three *Te Deums,* in D, B flat and A major.

38 Latin Church Music

I *Laudate pueri* A; II *Laudate pueri* B; III *Dixit Dominus;* IV *Nisi Dominus;* V *Salve Regina;* VI motet *Silete venti;* VII 6 *Allelujas.*

39 *La resurrezione* (Oratorio).

40 *Esther* (Oratorio) 1st version 1720 (*ie Haman and Mordecai,* a masque).

41 *Esther* (Oratorio) 2nd version, 1732.

42 *Joseph* (Oratorio).

43 *Occasional Oratorio.*

44 *Jephtha* (Oratorio).

45 *Messiah* (Oratorio) (co-editor M Seiffert).

46 (A) Ode for the birthday of Queen Anne.

(B) *Alceste* (' Musical scenes to an English play ').

47 (A) *Water Music, Firework Music,* concertos and double concertos.

(B) Supplement to above.

48 A miscellaneous collection of instrumental music.

I: 6 organ concertos ('Second set'); 3 organ concertos in D minor, and F major.

II: overture to *Orestes;* overture to *Alessandro Severo;* overture in B flat; sonata for viola da gamba and concertante harpsichord; sonata (VI) for 2 violins and bass; 3 sonatas for flute and continuo (nos. XVI-XVIII); *Sinfonie diverse,* for orchestra; hornpipe for Vauxhall.

III: Keyboard music and arrangements *Klavierbuch aus der Jugendzeit,* including the *Suite à deux clavecins;* 6 little fugues; lesson in A; overture in *Il Pastor fido,* arrangement for keyboard; aria ('Dolce bene') in *Radamisto* for keyboard; aria ('Vo' far guerra') in *Rinaldo* for keyboard; W Babell's *Rinaldo* arrangements.

49 Never published in its entirety (but three of the 'Deutsche Arien' were issued in 1959 by Moeck Verlag, Celle from the original plates).

50 and 51 73 cantatas for solo voice and bass. A full list of titles is given in Grove 1954, vol IV, page 55, and in CB 25.

52 A and B 28 cantatas, the last four fragmentary, for various voices and instruments. A full list of titles is given in Grove 1954, vol IV, pages 55, 56 and in CB 24.

Vols 55 to 94 are all operas, except vol 84, *Terpsicore,* which is a prologue to the second version of *Il Pastor fido.*

53 *Aci, Galatea e Polifemo* (serenata).

54 *Il Parnasso in festa* (serenata).

55 *Almira.*

56 *Rodrigo.*

57 *Agrippina.*

58 *Rinaldo* (1st and 2nd version) (two editions).

59 *Il Pastor fido* (1st version).

60 *Teseo.*

61 *Silla.*

62 *Amadigi.*

63 *Radamisto.*

64 *Muzio Scevola,* act 3.

65 *Floridante.*

66 *Ottone.*

67 *Flavio.*

68 *Giulio Cesare.*

69 *Tamerlano.*

70 *Rodelinda.*	85 *Ariodante.*
71 *Scipione.*	86 *Alcina.*
72 *Alessandro.*	87 *Atalanta.*
73 *Admeto.*	88 *Giustino.*
74 *Riccardo primo.*	89 *Arminio.*
75 *Siroe.*	90 *Berenice.*
76 *Tolomeo.*	91 *Faramondo.*
77 *Lotario.*	92 *Serse.*
78 *Partenope.*	93 *Imeneo.*
79 *Poro.*	94 *Deidamia.*
80 *Ezio.*	95 *Jephtha,* facsimile of the autograph score.
81 *Sosarme.*	
82 *Orlando.*	96 *Messiah,* facsimile of the autograph score.
83 *Arianna.*	
84 *Terpsicore.*	

REPRINTS OF HG

Chrysander's edition was resurrected *in toto* when it was reprinted in 1965-66 by the Gregg Press of Ridgewood, New Jersey, USA, and Farnborough, Hampshire. The format was reduced by about one third, and some of the more slender original volumes were issued as double numbers, bound in one, as follows (the titles are given in the preceding list): 3 and 6; 9 and 15; 23 and 18; 24 and 20; 31 and 11; 40 and 41; 46a and b; 56 and 61; 59 and 84; 87 and 64.

An earlier and more selective reprint of HG, reduced to miniature score format, was produced by Lea Pocket Scores (Universal Edition, NY and London). It comprised mostly instrumental works and the volumes are listed, under the abbreviation LPS, in the section ' other editions '.

HG supplements (works of other composers used by Handel) 1 Erba, *Magnificat,* 2 Urio, *Te Deum,* 3 Stradella, *Serenata,* 4 Clari, *Duetti,* 5 Muffat, *Componimenti Musicali,* 6 Keiser, *Octavia.*

THE ' HALLISCHE HÄNDEL-AUSGABE '—THE HALLE HANDEL EDITION

By the early 1950s, Chrysander's Händel-Gesellschaft edition was becoming increasingly difficult to obtain, even secondhand. Editorial standards had also greatly changed in the half-century since his death, and what contented the nineteenth century was no longer satisfactory to the mid-twentieth. A new edition was therefore proposed, under the auspices of the Georg Friedrich Händel-Gesellschaft and in association with Bärenreiter Verlag of Kassel and London, the general editors being Max Schneider and Rudolf Steglich. The edition was to be arranged in series, according to the type of work involved, as follows:

Series I Oratorios and large-scale cantatas
II Operas
III Church music
IV Instrumental music
V Smaller vocal works

Publication began in 1955 and although there was some rather severe criticism of the earliest volumes (from the point of view of modern scholarship), it is widely accepted that generally the new edition, known as HHA, is a considerable improvement on the old HG edition, if only because the critical notes to each volume, issued in a parallel series of *Kritische Berichte* are much fuller and more informative than were Chrysander's prefaces. He did not issue separate volumes of critical commentary at all. The main criticism levelled against the first two or three volumes in the HHA edition was that the editors had not consulted the entire range of source materials, especially the secondary manuscript sources. The editors of some of the later volumes have, however, virtually swung to the opposite extreme.

The following volumes had been issued by the end of 1970 (an asterisk against a volume indicates that it is also obtainable as a Bärenreiter miniature score; a double asterisk against a vocal work indicates that a vocal score is obtainable):

Series 1 Oratorios, etc

Vol 1, *Alexander's Feast** (K Ameln). Vol 2, *Passion according to St John* (K G Fellerer). Vol 6 *Ode for Queen Anne's Birthday** (W Siegmund-Schultze). Vol 7, *Brockes Passion* (F Schroeder). Vol 13, *Saul** (P Young) Vol 16 *L'Allegro, il penseroso ed il moderato* (J S Hall and M Hall). Vol 17, *Messiah** ** (J Tobin). Vol 28, *Susanna* (B Rose). Vol 31, *The choice of Hercules** (W Siegmund-Schultze).

Series II Operas

Vol 14, *Giulio Cesare** (F Zschoch). Vol 26, *Ezio** (Zschoch). Vol 28, *Orlando* (S Flesch). Vol 32, *Ariodante** (Siegmund-Schultze). Vol 39, *Serse** (R Steglich).

Series III Church music

Vol 1, Dixit Dominus* (E Wenzel).

Series IV Instrumental music

Vol 1, keyboard music I. suites 1-8 (Steglich). Vol 2, 6 organ concertos, op 4 (K Matthaei). Vol 3, 11 sonatas for flute and figures bass (H P Schmitz). Vol 4, 6 sonatas for violin and figures bass (J P Hinnenthal). Vol 5, keyboard music II (P Northway). Vol 6, keyboard music III (T M G Best). Vol 10 part 1, 9 sonatas for 2 violins and continuo, op 2 (S Flesch). Vol 10 part 2, 7 sonatas for 2 violins and continuo, op 5 (Flesch). Vol 11, 6 concert grossi, op 3* (F Hudson). Vol 13, *Water Music* and *Music for the Royal Fireworks** (H F Redlich), Vol 14, 12 concerti grossi, op 6* (A Hoffmann and Redlich).

It is planned to issue vocal scores with piano reductions for all the vocal works. The instrumental works are issued in parts as well as score. The full scores issued in the HHA series are all folio. Performing material for the operas, oratorios, etc is usually available from Bärenreiter at 32 Great Titchfield Street, London W1. In the case of the instrumental works, separate parts are issued as well as scores, and for vols 3 and 4 of series IV (the sonatas for solo instrument and continuo) a useful 'Dublierstimme' part is issued which leaves the figured bass unrealised and accordingly provides some useful practice material for the would be continuo player.

OTHER EDITIONS

In the following lists, when no town is given the place of publication is London. The place of publication and the editor's initials are omitted when either recurs several times in succession. Publishers' addresses are most readily available in the *British catalogue of music* (issued by the British National Bibliography) which is to be found in major public libraries throughout the world. Besides the addresses of all British music publishers, this catalogue includes those of the leading American firms and those of many European firms which have branches or agencies in London.

The following lists are not meant to be exhaustive, as the number of editions of Handel's music is immense and the mere listing of them would require a much larger book than the present one. The general principles of selection may be outlined as follows: scholarly quality and the consequent value of the text or editorial preface or of both; the historical interest of the editor or arranger as a famous performer or teacher; the fact that a work (for example, the vocal score of an opera) may not have been otherwise issued in that form; the interest of an arrangement, in an unusual but convenient medium. In addition to well-edited pocket or miniature scores, other useful ones without editor's name have also been included.

It cannot be too strongly emphasised that the presence of a title in these lists is not necessarily an indication of its present availability. Even the most recent editions have an unpredictable and unfortunate way of going out of print almost overnight, and in the case of anything issued before, for example, 1950 (to take only a convenient date) the chances are that it may well not be available for purchase. Therefore the earlier the edition, the more likely become the chances of non-availability. Nevertheless, it is worth remembering that anyone resident in Great Britain may be able to obtain out of print music on loan from the Central Music Library (Buckingham Palace Road, London SW1), to which application may be made direct or through the local public library.

The following abbreviations are used for the names of publishers:

Bä =Bärenreiter	LPS=Lea Pocket Scores
Br =Breitkopf and Härtel	OUP=Oxford University Press
Eul =Eulenburg	PH =Peters/Hinrichsen
GT =Goodwin & Tabb	UE =Universal Edition
NMA =Neue Mozart Ausgabe	UMP=United Music Publishers
Nov=Novello	

Other abbreviations are:

arr =arranged by	HG =Händel-Gesellschaft
CB =Craig Bell	HHA=Hallische Händel Ausgabe
ed =edited, or edition by	*min sc*=miniature score
fs =full score	o/h =on hire

orch = orchestra   ser = series
org = organ   str   = string or strings
pub = published   *vs*   = vocal score

The scheme of arrangement is as follows:

I Vocal Music

1 Operas and pasticcios (arranged alphabetically)
2 Oratorios, masques, serenatas, odes (arranged alphabetically)
3 Secular music for voices
  (a) Italian cantatas with instruments
  (b) Italian cantatas with continuo
  (c) Chamber duets and trios with Latin words
  (d) Cantatas with words in languages other than Latin
4 German sacred music
5 Latin motets, psalms, etc
6 English anthems and psalms
7 English liturgical music
8 English hymns

II Instrumental Music

1 Orchestral
  (a) Oboe concertos
  (b) Concerti grossi, op 3
  (c) Concerti grossi, op 6
  (d) Organ concertos, op 4, 7
  (e) Occasional music
  (f) Miscellaneous orchestral works
2 Chamber music
  (a) Solo sonatas, for melody instrument with continuo, op 1
  (b) Trio sonatas, op 2, 5, etc
3 Keyboard music
  (a) Suites
  (b) Miscellaneous
4 Miscellaneous
  Clock music

For identification I have, in each case, added the CB number (see page 57). Editions of a work are listed in the following sequence:
Full scores

Miniature scores
Vocal scores
Orchestral extracts (overtures, etc)
  (a) Full and miniature scores
  (b) Piano solo reductions
  (c) Piano duo and/or duet
  (d) Organ arrangements

I VOCAL MUSIC

I.1 Operas and pasticcios

Admeto (CB 34): *fs* HG 73.

Agrippina (CB 34): *fs* HG 57; *vs* H C Wolff (Bä). Overture: (Br); o/h (GT); sinfonia, by Wolff o/h (Bä).

Alcina (CB 101): *fs* HG 86. Overture and dances ('Festive music') (Möseler, Wolfenbüttel). Overture only: ed R Jacques (OUP); 'Il Ballo' ed W G Whittaker (OUP).

Alessandro (CB 73): *fs* HG 72. Overture (Möseler, Wolfenbüttel).

Alessandro Severo (pasticcio) (CB s8 (1)). Overture: arr for string orch by A Collins (Francis, Day & Hunter).

Almira (CB 9): *fs* HG 55, *vs* J N Fuchs (Kistner, Leipzig). Chaconne: arr for wind quartet by H Aaron (Schirmer).

Amadigi (CB 46): *fs* HG 62.

Arianna (CB 93): *fs* HG 83. Overture: o/h (GT); Lehmann o/h (Bä).

Ariodante (CB 100): *fs* HG 85; HHA ser II (32), by K J Furth (Bä); *vs* W Siegmund-Schultze (Bä). Overture: Siegmund-Schultze o/h (Bä).

Arminio (CB 109): *fs* HG 89. Overture: arr for organ by H Ley (Stainer & Bell, Reigate).

Atalanta (CB 106): *fs* HG 87.

Berenice (CB 107): *fs* HG 90. Overture (Möseler, Wolfenbüttel): arr string orch by G Bantock, o/h (GT).

Deidamia (CB 126): *fs* HG 94; *vs* by R Steglich o/h (Bä).

Ezio (CB 86): *fs* HG 80; HHA ser II, 26 by H Ruckert (Bä); *vs* by Zschoch (Bä); by P Kickstat (Göttingen University Press). Overture: Zschoch o/h (Bä).

Faramondo (CB 114): *fs* HG 91. Overture: arr str orch H Rawlinson (the editor, London); by A Collins (Francis, Day & Hunter).

Flavio (CB 67): *fs* HG 67.

Floridante (CB 63): *fs* HG 65; *vs* by Gervinus (Br). ' Quando pena la costanza ', facsimile of the autograph (privately printed, London).

Giulio Cesare (Julius Caesar) (CB 69): *fs* HG 68; HHA ser II, 14 by W Giesler (Bä); *vs* by Zschoch (Bä) revised for the stage by O Hagen; English translation by B Q Morgan (Peters). Overture: arr str orch by G Bantock, o/h (GT).

Giustino (Justin) (CB 108): *fs* HG 88.

Imeneo (Hymen) (CB 118): *fs* HG 93 (overture).

Jupiter in Argos (*Perseus and Andromeda*) (CB 119). No *fs*: published in vocal score only, as *Perseus and Andromeda*: an operatic masque by A G Latham, with music taken from a hitherto unpublished opera entitled *Jupiter in Argos*, transcribed and prepared by J Herbage and R Greaves under the supervision of A Boult (OUP).

Lotario (CB 80): *fs* HG 77.

Music Scevola (CB 62) act III only by Handel: *fs* HG 64.

Orlando (CB 91): *fs* HG 82: HHA ser II, 28 by S Flesch (Bä). Overture: ed G Frotscher (Bä).

Ottone (CB 64): *fs* HG 66; *vs* by O Hagen (R Chrysander, Bergedorf, 1925). Overture: ed R Jacques (OUP); G Bantock o/h (GT); arr organ solo by P Williams (Cramer).

Parnasso in festa, 11 (CB 99): *fs* HG 54. Overture: arr str orch by A Collins (Francis, Day & Hunter).

Partenope (CB 83): *fs* HG 78.

Pastor fido, Il, Version 1 (CB 39): *fs* HG 59. Overture: A Wenzinger, o/h (Bä). Suite: ed G Frotscher (Sikorski, Hamburg). Version II (CB 96): *fs* HG 84. Suite: (Mirtillo-Suite) arr A Schering (Kahnt, Leipzig).

Perseus and Andromeda see *Jupiter in Argos.*

Poro (CB 84): *fs* HG 79. Overture: arr organ by C S Lang (Nov).

Ptolemy see *Tolomeo.*

Radamisto (CB 57): *fs* HG 63.

Riccardo primo (CB 75): *fs* HG 74. Overture: arr for organ by C S Lang (Nov).

Rinaldo (CB 37): *fs* HG 58. Overture, symphonies and dances (Möseler, Wolfenbüttel).

Rodelinda (CB 71): *fs* HG 70; *vs arr* O Hagen (PH); Lehmann (Bä). Overture: *min sc* (with suite from *Terpsicore*) (Eul); also W Danckert o/h (Bä); also o/h (GT).

Rodrigo (CB 23): *fs* HG 56. Overture and dances: arr A Lewis and P Cranmer (OUP). Suite: arr Danckert (Nagel, Kassel).

Scipione (CB 72): *fs* HG 71. Overture: arr organ by P Williams (Cramer).

Serse (CB 115): *fs* HG 92; HHA ser II, 39 ed R Steglich (Bä); *vs* Steglich (Bä); E Wolff (PH); O Hagen (PH). Sinfonia, aria and gigue (Corona 35, Möseler, Wolfenbüttel).

Silla (CB 45): *fs* HG 61.

Siroe (CB 78). Overture: F W Cowen (Curwen); also o/h (GT).

Sosarme (CB 87): *fs* HG 81. Overture: arr for organ by C S Lang (Nov).

Tamerlano (CB 70): *fs* HG 69; *vs* arr H Roth (Br).

Terpsicore (CB 97): *fs* HG 84. Suite: ed H Müller; *min sc* (Eul): parts available in ' Praeclassica ' series (Eul).

Teseo (*Theseus*) (CB 40): *fs* HG 60; *vs* R Gerber (Bä). Overture: ed R Gerber o/h (Bä); arr str orch by H Rawlinson (the editor, London); arr solo organ by C S Lang (Nov).

Tolomeo (*Ptolemy*) (CB 79): *fs* HG 76. Overture: ed G Bantock o/h (GT); arr organ C S Lang (Nov).

Xerxes see *Serse*.

I.2 Oratorios, masques, serenatas, odes

Aci, Galatea e Polifemo (CB 33): *fs* HG 53.

Acis and Galatea (CB 56): *fs* HG 3; no editor (PH); arr Mozart (Bä); *vs* over-edited J Barnby (Nov); G Gervinus (PH). Overture: o/h (GT). Piano duo: arr R B Miller (OUP).

Alceste (CB 152) (sometimes known as *Alcides*): *fs* HG 46B; *vs* (Nov). Overture: arr for organ by W D Pearson (PH).

Alexander Balus (CB 114): *fs* HG 33.

Alexander's Feast (CB 103): *fs* HG 12; HHA ser I, 1 K Ameln (Bä); arr Mozart, ed A Holschneider; NMA ser X, 28,3 (Bä); arr Mozart (PH); trs ed K Ameln (Bä); arr V Novello (Nov); arr F Brissler (PH). Overture: arr for str orch by G Bantock o/h (GT); arr for organ by L Lazell (Lengnick).

L'Allegro, il penseroso ed il moderato (CB 123): *fs* HG 6; HHA ser I,16 ed J S and M V Hall (Bä); *vs* ed W H Monk (Nov); ed H Bornefeld (Bä); ed Hall (Bä).

Athalia (CB 94): *fs* HG 5; *vs* ed A Lewis (OUP); (Nov). Overture: arr F G Walker (Bosworth); also o/h (GT).

Belshazzar (CB 139): *fs* HG 19; ed J Spengel (PH); *vs* ed G Macfarren (Nov); the same, though abridged (Nov); W Brückner-Ruggeberg (PH).

Choice of Hercules, The (CB 154): *fs* HG 18; HHA ser I, 31 ed W Siegmund-Schultze (Bä); *vs* arr N Stone (Nov); arr Siegmund-Schultze (Bä).

Deborah (CB 92): *fs* HG 29; *vs* arr V Novello (Nov).

Esther (1720 version, CB 59): *fs* HG 40.

Esther (1732 version, CB 89): *fs* HG 41; *vs* ed C Lucas (Nov). Overture: arr A Carse (Augener-Galliard); O Sommer (Vieweg, Berlin); also o/h (GT).

Hercules (CB 138): *fs* HG 4; *vs ed* E Prout (Nov). Overture: ed A Schering (Kahnt, Leipzig; also o/h (GT).

Israel in Egypt (CB 117): *fs* HG 16; ed A Dörffel (PH) *vs* ed Mendelssohn, arr V Novello (Nov); arr F Brissler, (PH).

Jephtha (CB 156): *fs* facsimile of Handel's autograph, published for the German Handel Society on his bicentenary (F Chrysander, Bergedorf, 1885); HG 44; *vs* ed V Novello (Nov); arr C Neher and G Rennert, for the stage (Bä).

Joshua (CB 145): *fs* HG 17 ed Dörffel (PH); *vs* ed E Prout (Nov); arr J Stern (PH).

Joseph and his Brethren (CB 137): *fs* HG 42; *vs* arr M Seiffert (Dreissig, Hamburg).

Judas Maccabaeus (CB 143): *fs* HG 22; ed A Dörffel (PH).

Judas Maccabaeus has understandably always been one of the most popular of all Handel's oratorios, there have been many vocal scores. Here I can only quote one or two of the best known. The most generally popular are: arr by J E West (Nov); a German edition arr by J Stern (PH); a French one arr by C Lamoureux (Heugel, Paris). Overture: o/h (GT); arr for organ solo by W Pearson (OUP).

Messiah (CB 130). There are two facsimiles of Handel's autograph score. The first, which was not quite complete, was issued by the Sacred Harmonic Society in 1868, the second being prepared by Chrysander (Strumper, Hamburg, 1892). The latter is complete and the more accurate of the two, but it failed to overcome many of the problems of exact reproduction of minutiae. There is also *Selection from the original manuscript of the Messiah* prepared by O E Deutsch (Heffer, Cambridge, ' Harrow Replicas ' 8).

fs: HG 45. For some curious reason, perhaps because of its very popularity, Chrysander delayed the publication of his HG *Messiah* score, so that eventually it was issued posthumously, and seen through the press by M Seiffert (1902). Other celebrated full scores are HHA ser I, 17 edited by J Tobin (Bä); ed Watkins Shaw (Nov); a much earlier Novello score was that by T W Bourne, which claimed to follow ' the original edition ' (Nov 1899); Alfred Mann has also edited a good clean version of the score, issued in 3 vols (Rutgers University Press, New Brunswick, NJ). Mozart's famous (or should one say notorious?) ' additional accompaniments ' have appeared in several versions, the most recent being that in the *Neue Mozart Ausgabe* ser X, 28, vol 2 edited by A Holschneider (Bä). Mozart's version can also be seen in a PH score, and is somewhat horribly reinforced by the famous Robert Franz in a now mercifully out of print edition by Kistner of Leipzig in 1884. Franz's most notable effort in this version was to bring back the main theme of ' Every valley ' as a kind of Wagnerian leitmotiv, played on the horns, in the aria *Rejoice greatly O daughter of Zion*!

min sc: miniature scores of *Messiah* are available from Bärenreiter following Tobin's HHA edition, and from Eulenberg, ed by F Vollbach. The number of *Messiah* vocal scores is overwhelming, even more numerous than those of *Judas Maccabaeus*. I can only list a few of them, the most immediately useful and trustworthy one, for the English musician, being that by Watkins Shaw (Nov), closely followed by J Tobin's (Bä) issued in conjunction with his HHA full score. (The older Novello vocal scores edited by V Novello and W T Best have now been rendered out of date by Shaw's.) An earlier attempt at a vocal score to match modern methods with Handel's practice was the vocal score of A Schering and K Soldan, based on the autograph and on the Foundling Hospital material,

73

with English and German words, published by Peters in Frankfurt in 1939 and reprinted in 1955 (PH). One very interesting vocal score was that ' edited from the original sources ' by the late J M Coopersmith, a great Handel scholar (Carl Fischer, NY). There is also an ' organ vocal score ' arr J Stein (PH). Overture etc: o/h (GT); with Pastoral Symphony, arr J Brown (Stainer & Bell, Reigate): arr organ (manuals only) by Watkins Shaw (Nov): Pastoral Symphony only, arr organ by A G Matthew (Cramer).

Occasional Oratorio (CB 141): *fs* HG 43. It is curious that a vocal score of this rare work was issued, ed by J Bishop, by Robert Cocks, as early as 1856. Novello's edition seems to have been somewhat later. There is also a German one by F Stein, (Bä). Overture : (Boosey); also o/h (GT); arr organ by H Coleman (Bosworth); by H Edmundson (H W Gray/Nov). Various pianoforte arrangements have been issued in the past.

Ode for the Birthday of Queen Anne (CB 43): *fs* HG 46A; HHA ser 6, ed W Siegmund-Schultze (Bä); *vs* arr Siegmund-Schultze (Bä).

Ode for St Cecilia's Day (CB 120): *fs* HG 23; also as a *min sc* in LPS no 164; arr Mozart, ed Holschneider NMA, X 28, 4 (Bä); *vs* with historical notes by F G Edwards (Nov); arr Chrysander (the editor, Bergedorf).

Resurrezione, La (CB 31): *fs* HG 39.

Samson (CB 31): *fs* HG 10; ed and abridged Prout (Nov); *vs* ed and abridged Prout (Nov); by H Kretschmar (PH). Overture: o/h (GT).

Saul (CB 116): *fs* HG 13; HHA ser I,13, ed P M Young (Bä). Overture: o/h (GT), arr organ by H Coleman (Cramer).

Semele (CB 134): *fs* HG 7; *vs* ed and abridged E Prout (Nov); ed A Rahlwes (Leuckart). Overture: o/h (GT).

Solomon (CB 146): *fs* HG 26; *vs* no editor (Nov); ed K Straube (Br); no editor (PH). Overture: ed Schering (Kahnt); arr str orch by J Brown (Stainer & Bell, Reigate), arr organ by H Coleman (Bosworth). The highly popular symphony to Act 3 ('Arrival of the Queen of Sheba ') has been arranged for all sorts of media; a few of them are listed below: orchestral version; arr str orch by R Jacques (OUP); piano solo: K Palmer (Paxton); R Müller-Hartmann (PH); piano duet: G Bryan (Chester); W Weissmann (PH); piano duo (*ie* 2 pianos): B Easdale (OUP); organ solo: J S Archer (Paxton); M Hicks (Ashdown); Stainton de B Taylor (PH); A G Matthew (Cramer).

Susanna (CB 147): *fs* HG 1; HHA ser I, 28, ed B Rose (Bä); *vs* no editor (Nov); ed B Rose (Bä); ed Gervinus (PH).

Theodora (CB 151): *fs* HG 8; *vs* ed A Lewis (Nov, replacing an older edition by G Macfarren); no editor (PH). Overture (Möseler, Wolfenbüttel).

Trionfo del tempo e del disinganno (CB 32): *fs* HG 32a.

Trionfo del tempo e della verità (CB 112—second version of CB 32): *fs* HG 20.

Triumph of Time and Truth, The (CB 157—English version of the above): *fs* HG 20; *vs* ed and rev E Prout (Nov); no editor (Leuckart).

I.3 Secular music for voices
I.3 (a)

Italian cantatas with instruments (CB 24). Complete edition: HG 52 A/B. Single cantatas in recent editions:

Apollo e Dafne ('*La terra e liberata*') (CB 24, 16), elaborately scored, is almost an opera in itself. *Fs* HG 50A: *vs* ed as *Apollo and Daphne: a dramatic cantata*, by A Lewis, English words by G Dunn (Chester); *Crudel tiranno Amor* (CB 24, 10) ed H Zenck (Bä); *Cuopre tal volta il cielo* (CB 24, 11) ed Zenck (Bä); *Pensieri notturni de Filli* ('*Nell' dolce dell' oblio*') (CB 24, 17) ed Zenck (Bä); *Tra le fiamme* (CB 24, 21) ed Zenck (Bä); *Tu fidel? tu costante?* (CB 24, 22) ed Zenck (Bä); ed F Wasner (Schirmer); ed W Bergmann and E Hunt, with English words by N Platt ('In love's sweet oblivion') (Schott).

I.3 (b)

Italian cantatas with continuo (CR 25). Complete edition: HG 50/51. Single cantatas in recent editions:

Dalla guerra amorosa (CB 25, 8) ed Zenck (Bä); *Figli del mesto cor* (CB 25, 19) ed H Roth (Euterpe, Stuttgart); *Lucrezia* ('*O numi eterni!*') (CB 25, 46) ed M Tippett and W Bergmann (Schott); *La bella pastorella* (CB 158) ed W H Cummings (only known ed, C Lonsdale, 1877).

I.3 (c)

Chamber duets and trios with Italian words (CB 29, 36, 133). Complete edition: HG 32; nos 2-7 of the duets revised by Brahms (PH). Facsimile of the autograph CB 133, no 2 *Quel fior che all' alba ride* (Drei Masken Verlag, Munich).

I.3 (d)

Cantatas with words in languages other than Italian

Spanish

No se emendera jamas (' Cantata Spagnuola a voce sola e chitarra ') (CB 24, 18). Complete edition: HG 52B; ed P van der Staak (Broelmans, Amsterdam).

French

7 airs françois (CB 28): (1) ' Sans y penser '; (2) ' Si'l ne falloit '; (3) ' Petite fleur brunette '; (4) ' Vous qui m'aviez '; (5) ' Nos plaisirs '; (6) ' Vous ne scauriez '; (7) ' Non, je ne puis suffrir '. The autograph of these interesting little pieces is in the British Museum (RM 20 d 11, fol 61-66). Nothing is known of their origin, and the only known edition of any of them (nos 6 and 7) was published in London (Lonsdale, *c* 1850).

English

Look down, harmonious saint (' In praise of St Cecilia ') (CB 24, 8); cantata for tenor and str orch, derived from the Italian cantata *Cecilia, volgi un sguardo* (CB 24, 6); *fs* HG 52A ed D Stevens (Pennsylvania State University); also ed M Seiffert as *Der Preis der Tonkunst* (Kistner & Siegel, Leipzig). *Venus and Adonis* (CB 38). Fragment, words by John Hughes. Not in HG. The only edition ed by W C Smith and Havergal Brian (Augener/Galliard).

3 English Cantatas (CB ?3); (1) ' To lovely shades '; (2) ' With roving and ranging '; (3) ' So pleasing the pains '. Not in HG. Manuscript copy in Biblioteca Santa Cecilia, Rome. Unpublished. Probably spurious.

The following songs with English words were printed in the eighteenth century but have remained largely unpublished in modern times; I place them in their CB order, for ease of reference:

CB 107: *Not, Cloe, that I better am* (Walsh, *c* 1736); CB 111: *I like*

76

the am'rous youth that's free (1st ed *c* 1737; also Walsh, 1741);
CB 122: *The death of the stag* ('When Phoebus the tops') issued in
various sheet song eds, *c* 1740 onwards; CB 124: *Love's but the
frailty of the mind,* ed A H Mann in *The early English musical
magazine* vol I, no 6 1891; CB 128: *Yes, I'm in love* (authenticity
somewhat doubtful), sheet song eds, *c* 1740 onwards; CB 140: *Stand
around, my brave boys* ('A song made for the Gentlemen Volun-
teers of the City of London), Simpson, 1745; CB 142: *From scourg-
ing rebellion* ('A song on the Victory obtained over the Rebels by
His Royal Highness The Duke of Cumberland'), words by Lockman
(Walsh, 1746); CB 155: *Hunting song* ('The morning is charming'),
the words by Handel's friend Charles Legh, of Adlington Hall,
Cheshire, where the autograph is still preserved. First published in
The early English musical magazine, vol I, no 6; also arr A H Mann
for SATB, ed O E Deutsch in *The musical times,* December 1942.

A large number of songs by Handel, with English words, were
printed in the eighteenth century, but most of these were adaptations
of arias in his Italian operas, or dance tunes from the same source,
and so do not qualify as original English songs.

I.4 German sacred music

The Brockes passion (CB 50): *fs* HG 15; HHA ser I, 7 ed F S Schroeder
(Bä); *vs* ed Schroeder (Bä); ed D Darlow (OUP); translated (horribly!) by the Rev J Troutbeck, who apologised in his preface for
doing it so badly (Nov).

The Passion after St John (CB ?10): is now regarded as being the
work of G Böhm—*see The musical times,* July, 1967; HG 9.

3 deutsche Lieder (CB 2): (1) 'In deinem schönen Mund';
(2) 'Endlich muss Man''; (3) Ein hoher Geist'. Not in HG. First ed
(Moeck, Celle), from HG plates (*see* page 63). No 3 only (Br).

9 deutsche Arien (CB 81): (1) 'Kunft'ger Zeiten'; (2) 'Das
zitternde Glänzen'; (3) Süsser Blumen'; (4) 'Süsse Stille, sanfte
Quelle'; (5) 'Singe, Seele, Gott zum Preise'; (6) 'Meine Seele hört
im Scheu'; (7) 'Die ihr aus dunkeln Grüften'; (8) 'In den angeneh-
men Büschen'; (9) 'Flammende Rose'. Not in HG. First ed by
E Roth (Drei Masken Verlag, Munich); practical ed (Br).

I.5 Latin motets, psalms, etc

Dixit dominus in G minor (CB 13): *fs* HG 38; HHA ser III, 1, ed E Wenzel (Bä); *vs* ed E Wenzel (Bä); arr S Taylor (Nov).

Laudate pueri dominum in D major (CB 14). Version 1, 1703 (CB 3); *fs* HG 38. Version 2, 1707 (CB 14); *fs* HG 38; also arr F Stein o/h (PH); *vs* arr Stein (PH).

Nisi dominus and *Gloria patri* in G major (CB 15): *fs* HG 38 *Nisi dominus* only; *Gloria patri*, from score in Nanki Library, Tokyo (Nanki, 1928).

Salve regina in G mi (CB 16): *fs* HG 38; ed Seiffert (Br). Complete work (Nov).

Haec est regina virginum, antiphon (CB 17): unpublished.

Te decus virginum, antiphon (CB 18): unpublished.

Seuiat tellus inter vigores, motet (CB 19): unpublished.

Donna che in ciel, motet with Italian text (CB 20): (Arno Volk Verlag (Cologne); ed R Ewerhart (Bieler, Cologne).

Coelestis dum spirat aura, antiphon (CB 21): ed R Ewerhart (Bieler).

O qualis de coelo sonus, antiphon (CB 22): ed Ewerhart (Bieler).

6 Allelujahs (CB 160): *fs* HG 38.

Silete venti, motet (CB 82): HG 38.

I.6 English anthems and psalms

Chandos anthems (CB 52, 1-11):

(1) *O be joyful in the Lord;* (2) *In the Lord put I my trust;* (3) *Have mercy upon me;* (4) & (4a) *O sing unto the Lord a new song;* (5) & (5a) *I will magnify Thee;* (6) & 6a-d) *As pants the hart;* (7) *My song shall be alway;* (8) *O come let us sing unto the Lord;* (9) *O praise the Lord with one consent;* (10) *The Lord is my light;* (11a, b) *Let God arise.*

The above numbering is that of Chrysander and HG; other publishers give different numbering. The choruses are often rearranged. *fs* HG 34-36; *vs* to separate anthems: (4) *O sing unto the Lord*, ed for 4 part chorus by S Adler (Chappell), SAB version (PH); (6) *As pants the hart*, STB version (PH), and ed K Fiebig and M Schneider (Merseburger, Berlin), ed S Adler (Chappell); (7) *My song shall be alway*, SATB version (PH); (8) *O come let us sing*, ed B Haynes (Nov);

(9) *O praise the Lord,* ed E Silas, with voice parts somewhat re-arranged (Nov), ed Seiffert (Br).

Overtures: (2) arr str orch by P James (Ricordi, NY), arr full orch by Elgar (Nov); 10 arr for organ by C S Lang (Nov).

Coronation anthems (CB 76, 1-4):

(1) *Zadok the Priest;* (2) *Let Thy hand be strengthened;* (3) *The King shall rejoice;* (4) *My heart is inditing; fs* HG 14 *min sc* LPS no 165; *vs* complete, ed E Silas (Nov); (Schirmer, NY). Singly: no 1, ed W Herrmann (Chappell); (Nov) (Br); arr TTBB by L Woodgate (Paterson); no 2 (Nov); ed W Herrmann (Schirmer, NY); no 3, 4 part and 6 part versions (Nov); 6 part version ed W Herrmann (Schirmer); No 4 (Nov).

Various single anthems, settings of psalms, etc.

Foundling Hospital anthem (*Blessed are they that consider the poor*) (CB 150): *fs* HG 36; *vs* no editor (PH).

Funeral anthem for Queen Caroline (*The ways of Zion do mourn*) (CB 113): *fs* HG 11; ed M Seiffert, Veröffent lichungen der Händel-Gesellschaft, vol 1 (Br); *vs* no editor (Nov).

Psalm 103 (*O praise the Lord, ye angels of his*) (CB 68); *fs* HG 36; *vs* (UE).

Wedding anthem 1 (*This is the day*) (CB 98): *fs* HG 36.
Wedding anthem 2 (*Sing unto God*) (CB 105): *fs* HG 36; *vs* (Br).

I.7 English liturgical music

Utrecht Te Deum and *Jubilate* (CB 41) written to celebrate the Peace of Utrecht in 1713: *fs* HG 31; *vs* ed Watkins Shaw (Nov); (Merseburger, Berlin); (UE); (PH).

Dettingen Te Deum (CB 136) written to celebrate the victory at Dettingen in 1743; *fs* HG 25; ed K Straube and Seiffert (PH); *min sc* ed A D Walker (Eul); *vs* ed W Emery (Nov); ed Straube and Seiffert (PH).

Chandos Te Deums (CB 44, 55, 60): *fs* HG 37; *vs* CB 55; B flat version adapted J Barnby (Nov).

I.8 English hymns

3 Wesleyan hymn tunes (CB 153) for voice and organ: (1) O Love divine, how sweet Thou art (' Fitzwilliam '); (2) Rejoice the Lord is King (' Gopsal '); (3) Sinners, obey the gospel word (' Cannons ').

Not in HG. These three hymn tunes to words by C Wesley have survived in a single manuscript in the Fitzwilliam Museum. They were copied from that source and published by S Wesley in 1826. No 2 is very famous and can be found in many hymn books.

II INSTRUMENTAL MUSIC
II.1 ORCHESTRAL: **Oboe concertos**
II.1 (a)
3 Concertos for solo oboe and strings (CB 5, 1-3): *fs* HG 21; LPS no 54. Score and pts; arr Seiffert as Concerti Grossi nos 8-10 (Br); ed A Hoffmann (Möseler, Wolfenbüttel). Oboe and pf reductions: nos 1-3, arr A Willner (Boosey). No 3 in G minor: arr L Goossens and H Craxton (Br), arr A Wunderer (UE).

II.1 (b) Concertos op 3
Concerti grossi, op 3 ('The Hautboy Concertos' (CB 51): *fs* HG 21; HHA ser IV, 11, ed F Hudson (Bä); arr Seiffert, as Concerti Grossi nos 1-6 (Br); op 3 no 3 arr for recorder and str T Dart (OUP). *min sc*: LPS 54; ed F Hudson (Bä); ed S Sadie (Eul). Single nos op 3 no 2 in B flat: ed H Roth (Philharmonia/UE).

Concerto Grosso, op 3 no 4a in F major (no CB number). This work was published in the first (Walsh) edition of op 3, but was quickly removed and the present op 3 no 4 substituted for it. It seems to be of doubtful authenticity. It is not in HG, but is in HHA ser IV, 11, and also ed H F Redlich and F Hudson (Eul).

II.1 (c) Concerti grossi
12 Concerti grossi ('Grand Concertos') op 6, nos 1-12 (CB 121, 1-12): *fs* HG 30; HHA ser IV, 14, ed A Hoffmann and H F Redlich (Bä); ed W Weismann (PH); nos 2, 5, 10, ed G F Kogel (PH); ed and arr by Seiffert and others as Concerti Grossi nos 12-23 (Br); no editor (Kalmus). *min sc*: LPS no 71/2, ed Redlich and Hoffmann (Bä); ed G Schumann (Eul); no editor (Boosey & Hawkes). Nos 1, 5, 6, 10 (Ricordi); no 6 (Philharmonia/UE); nos 1 and 7, ed H May (Schott).

Concerto grosso in C major ('*Alexander's Feast*') for oboes and str (CB 104): *fs* HG 21; ed F Mottl for full symphony orch (PH). *min sc*: ed F Schroeder (Eul) and in LPS no 54.

II.1 (d) Organ concertos

Handel composed a number of organ concertos and their enumeration poses some problems. His 'First Set' of six (CB 102) was published in 1738 as his op 4. Some two years later Walsh published a 'Second Set' (CB S4), without opus number, and which was made up of two genuine organ concertos, plus four other concertos arranged from the op 6 Concerti Grossi. Then in 1761 a 'Third Set' (CB 129) appeared, assembled posthumously from his manuscripts. This does not exhaust the list, though; Chrysander published three in HG 48; one was a fragment of a concerto for two organs, strings and bassoons, in D minor, related to op 7, no 4; the second, in D minor, was 'borrowed' by Handel from a sonata in Telemann's *Musique de table* and the third was a huge concerto in F for solo organ, oboes, bassoons and strings, sometimes called 'The Concerto in *Judas Maccabaeus*' related to the *Concerti a due cori* in F (CB 176) published in HG 47 and 48. Seiffert numbered these concertos 1 to 16 for his complete Breitkopf edition and since this numbering is often, but not invariably used, it is quoted here.

The 16 Organ Concertos, complete in 2 vols, LPS nos 125-6, arr for solo organ by M Dupré, 3 vols (Bornemann, Paris, UMP).

6 Concertos for organ, harpsichord and orchestra, op 4 'First set' (CB 102: Seiffert nos 1-6): *fs* HG 28; HHA ser IV, 2 ed K Matthaei (Bä); arr Seiffert (Br); arr M Walcha (Schott). *min sc*: LPS no 125. Solo organ: concertos 1-6 arr C S Lang and J Dykes Bower (Nov); arr K Matthaei (manuals only) (Bä); arr H Keller with pedals, (Bä); S de Lange (PH); arr H Walcha with orch arranged as organ II (Schott); arr M Dupré (Bornemann, Paris, UMP). Piano duet: arr A Ruthardt (PH). Single concertos: op 4 no 6 (originally for harp) ed for harp by C Salzedo (Chappell); for piano (!) organ or harpsichord, arr W Hilleman (Nagel, Kassel). Concerto in B flat, selected and arr for pf and orch by C Lambert from op 4 nos 2, 6 (OUP).

6 concertos for organ, harpsichord and orchestra, op 7 'Third Set' (CB 129: Seiffert, nos 7-12): *fs* HG 28; arr Seiffert (Br); arr H Walcha (Schott). *min sc*: LPS nos 125-6. Solo organ: arr H Keller, with pedals, (Bä); H Walcha, with orch (Schott); arr as organ II S De Lange (Schott); arr M Dupré (Bornemann, Paris, UMP). Piano duet: arr A Ruthardt (PH).

81

Concerto in F ('*The Cuckoo and the Nightingale*') 'Second Set no 1 ', (Seiffert no 13): *fs* HG 48; ed H Liedecke (Merseburger, Berlin); ed W Mohr (PH). *min sc*: LPS no 126. Solo organ: arr M Dupré (Bornemann, Paris, UMP); arr G Phillips (PH); arr E Power Biggs (H W Gray, NY). Piano solo: arr L Duck (Francis, Day & Hunter); arr Mohr (PH).

Concerto in A major, 'Second Set, no 2 ' (CB S4, 2: Seiffert no 14): *fs* HG 48 arr Seiffert (Br). *min sc*: LPS no 126. Organ solo: arr M Dupré (Bornemann, UMP); arr W Mohr, with orch as second keyboard (PH).

Concerto in D minor (fragment) (CB 180): *fs* HG 48; ed Mohr (PH). *min sc*: LPS no 126. Organ solo: arr M Dupré (Bornemann, UMP); arr W Mohr with orch as second keyboard (PH).

Concerto in D minor, after Telemann (CB 179: Seiffert no 15): *fs* HG 48; arr Seiffert (Br). *min sc*: LPS no 126. Organ solo: arr M Dupré (Bornemann, UMP); arr W Mohr, with orch as second keyboard (PH).

Concerto in F major for organ, oboes, horns, bassoons and strings ('Concerto in *Judas Maccabaeus*') (CB 176 C; Seiffert no 16): *fs* HG 48; arr Seiffert (Br); ed Mohr (PH). *min sc*: LPS no 126. Organ solo: arr M Dupré (Bornemann, UMP); arr W Mohr, with orch as second keyboard (PH).

II.1 (e) Occasional music

The *Water Music* (CB 47). The nature and origin of the *Water Music* are rather obscure and have been discussed on page 17. As the autograph is lost, both manuscript copies and early printed sources are important: their relative merits are discussed in the prefaces to the miniature scores listed below, in which some problems of scoring are also examined.

The *Water Music*: *fs* HG 47; HHA ser IV, 13 ed H F Redlich, with the *Fireworks Music* (Bä); arr M Seiffert as Concerto Grosso no 25 (Br). Selections: suite from the *Water Music,* ed A Baines (OUP); arr for modern symphony orchestra by Sir H Harty (Chappell). *min sc*: ed Redlich (Bä); ed B Priestman (Eul); LPS no 139. Selections: suite in F (Boosey & Hawkes, Heugel); suite in D, 'Mr Handel's waterpiece ' for trumpet, str and continuo; ed E H Tarr

(Musica Rara). Piano arrangements: ed J Pittman (Augener/Galliard); arr G Bantock (Paxton); ed E M Ripin (Chappell); Harty's version, arr G H Clutsam (Chappell). Selection: piano duet: arr L Duck (PH); arr A Richardson (OUP). Two pianos: arr P Tate (OUP). Organ: arr J S Archer (Paxton).

The *Music for the Royal Fireworks* (CB 53): although the autograph of the *Fireworks Music* is extant, there are some doubts about the exact instrumentation and about what forces were used in early performances. These and other similar points are dealt with in the prefaces to the miniature scores listed below. *fs* HG 47; HHA ser IV, 13, ed H F Redlich, with the *Water Music* (Bä); arr Seiffert as Concerto Grosso no 26 (Br); ed by A Baines and C MacKerras, for wind instruments only (OUP); ed R A Bondreau (Peters, NY); arr for concert band by H A Sartorius (Music Press, NY); arr by Sir Hamilton Harty for full symphony orch omitting the 'La Réjouissance' movement (Chappell); arr for brass band by D Wright (Richardson, Gloucester); arr D Stone for chamber orch (Nov). *min sc*: ed H F Redlich (Bä); LPS no 139, with the *Water Music*, etc; ed C L Cudworth (Eul); no editor (Boosey & Hawkes). Piano arrangements: arr G Bantock (Paxton); Harty's version, arr E Blom (Chappell). Organ: arr J S Archer (Paxton).

The *Forest Music* (CB 132). This very doubtful set of pieces, said to have been composed by Handel during his stay in Ireland, was first published in 1803 by F Rhames in Dublin, and there have been one or two reprints of it. The most recent arrangements are for organ by C Kingsbury (H W Gray Co, NY/Nov) and for harpsichord by I Kipnis in his *First harpsichord book* (OUP).

II.1 (f) Miscellaneous orchestral works (CB 148)

(a) *Concerto in F major,* (b) *Concerto in D,* both related to the *Fireworks Music. fs* HG 47: (a) only, ed A Schering (Kahnt, Leipzig). *min sc*: LPS no 140.

3 Concerti a due cori (CB 176) for oboes, bassoons, horns, strings, etc: *fs* HG 47 and 48. *min sc*: LPS no 140.

Concerto in D major for 2 horns and str orch (CB 42): ed M Seiffert as Concerto Grosso no 30 (Br), possibly spurious.

Concerto (sonata a 5) for solo violin and str orch (CB 35): *fs* HG

21. *min sc*: LPS no 54. Perf: ed arr Seiffert as Concerto Grosso no 11 (Br); also in Corona 74 (Möseler, Wolfenbüttel).

Concerto in E flat for solo oboe and str orch (CB 48): *fs* not in HG; first ed F Stein (Litolff); no editor (PH). Actually by R Woodcock.

Concerto for flute, str etc: ed A Hoffmann (Möseler).

Concerto for solo recorder, str etc: reconstructed W Bergmann from the recorder sonata op no 11 and organ concerto op 4 no 5 (Schott).

Concerto for 2 oboes, str etc (from manuscript Fu. 3741a in the Archbishop's Library in Paderborn): ed J P Hinnenthal (the author, Bielefeld).

Concerto in B minor for solo viola and orch (CB S2): arr H Casadesus (Eschig/Schott); undoubtedly spurious.

Suite for solo trumpet, oboes, bassoons, strings and continuo: ed Hinnenthal (the editor, Bielefeld).

Suite in G minor for flute, oboes, bassoon, strings: ed Hinnenthal (the editor, Bielefeld).

Suite with March (Corona 10, Möseler, Wolfenbüttel).

12 ' Symphonies ' (Corona 29, Möseler).

' Ouverture ' in B flat major, for oboes, str and continuo (CB 177): *fs* HG 48.

' Ouverture ' in D for flute, oboes, bassoons, archlute, strings and continuo (CB 178): autograph in British Museum, RM 20g 13, ff 29-32; unpublished.

Hornpipe for Vauxhall (CB 125) for strings: *fs* HG 48.

8 ' Sinfonie diverse ' (CB 184) short instrumental pieces, some identical with movements from the op 5 trio sonatas: *fs* HG 27 and 48.

Rigaudon, Bourrée and March for 2 oboes and bassoon: ed K Haas (Musica Rara); not in HG.

2 Arias for 2 oboes, 2 horns and bassoon (CB 167): ed K Haas (Musica Rara).

12 Marches for strings: ed R Steglich (Nagel Musik Archiv, no 108, Bä).

The Beecham arrangements: although we do not generally include modern re-orchestrations in these pages, it is felt that an exception must be made in the case of those by Sir Thomas

Beecham, since they are so famous (or infamous, depending on one's point of view!) that one cannot very well ignore them. The majority of Beecham arrangements were made up of dance-movements. The most celebrated of them are as follows: *The Gods go A-Begging*. Ballet suite (Cramer); *The Great Elopement* (*Love in Bath*), suites 1-2 (Mills); *The Faithful Shepherd Suite* mostly from *Pastor fido* II (Boosey); *Amaryllis,* mostly from *Alcina, Ariodante* and *Terpsicore* (Boosey).

II.2 CHAMBER MUSIC

As with the organ concertos, the numbering of Handel's chamber music is confusing, and for very similar reasons. The confusion began in the various editions published during his lifetime and subsequent editors, from Arnold and Chrysander onwards, have discovered and added new works in addition to the different versions of previously known ones.

For both groups in this section, it is probably simplest to list the works according to the numbering used by Seiffert in the practical edition he prepared for Breitkopf. His total of solo sonatas ran to nineteen and for the trio sonatas to twenty four. Other works in each group, which have been discovered since Seiffert's edition appeared, are listed at the end.

II.2 (a) Solo sonatas with continuo

Kammersonaten, ed M Seiffert, nos 1-15 ' op 1 ' (CB 65): nos 17, 18, 19. Flute sonatas; *fs* nos 1-19 only; HG 27 and 48. *min sc*: with all nineteen in one vol, LPS no 70 as *Nineteen sonatas for various instruments.*

6 Sonatas for violin and continuo (CB 65: Seiffert nos 4, 11, 13-16): HG 27; HHA ser IV, 4, ed J P Hinnenthal (Bä); ed Seiffert (Br). *min sc*: LPS no 70. Performing eds: Hinnenthal (Bä); ed H Sitt, 2 vol (PH); ed J B Colyns and F A Gevaert, 2 vols (Br); ed M Jacobsen (PH).

11 Sonatas for flute and continuo (CB 65: Seiffert nos 1 a b, 2, 4, 5, 7, 9, 11. (NB Sonatas nos 2, 4, 7, 11 were originally for the recorder): HG 27; HHA ser IV, 3 ed by H P Schmitz (Bä); ed Seiffert (Br). Other eds published by UE, Galliard, PH, Rudall Carte, etc.

Sonatas nos 2, 4, 7 & 11: ed for recorder and continuo by W Woehl (Rieter-Biedermann); by W Hillemann (Schott); by A Rodemann (Nagel, Kassel); transcribed oboe by W Tustin (Chappell).

3 'Halle sonatas' (CB 8: Seiffert 17-19) for flute and continuo: ed by W Woehl (PH).

Single sonatas: no 4 ed for recorder or flute and piano by A Dolmetsch (Associated Copyrights—London, 1935): sonatas nos 6, 8 for oboe and continuo (PH); sonata no 12 arr for oboe and piano by L Tertis (Hawkes); sonata no 15 arr for viola and piano by W Forbes and A Richardson (OUP).

Other sonatas: sonata for viola da gamba and concertante harpsichord (CB 7); 4 Fitzwilliam sonatas for recorder and continuo, ed T Dart (Schott); 3 'New sonatas' for recorder and continuo, ed W Danckert (Nagel); sonata in G minor for viola da gamba and harpsichord, ed T Dart (Schott).

II.2 (b) Trio sonatas, op 2, 5 etc

24 trio sonatas for 2 oboes, flutes or violins with continuo: HG 27, ed M Seiffert (Br) (nos 23 and 24 published for the first time).

6 Sonatas for 2 oboes and continuo (CB 1: Seiffert nos 1-6): HG 27; Seiffert (Br); nos 2, 3, 6 (International Music Corp, NY).

9 sonatas for 2 oboes, violins and continuo op 2 (CB 66: Seiffert nos 7-13): HG 27; HH3 ser IV, 9 ed S Flesch (Bä); ed W Kolneder (Schott). Selections: nos 3, 4, 6, 7, 8, 9 ed M Jacobsen (PH); nos 1, 4, 5, 6 ed L Moyse (Chappell). No 22 in D for flute, cello & harpsichord: ed Seiffert (Br). Single nos: trio-sonata no 23 in G minor for violin, gamba and harpsichord: ed Seiffert (Br). Op 2 no 4 arr recorder, violin and continuo A Rodemann (Nagel, Kassel).

7 sonatas for 2 violins, or German flutes with continuo, op 5 (CB S3: Seiffert nos 16-22): HG 27; HHA ser IV, 10, ed S Flesch (Bä); ed Seiffert (Br). Single sonatas: trio in F, op 5 no 2, for recorder, violin and continuo; ed W Upmeyer (Nagel).

Miscellaneous: *sonata in G minor for 2 flutes and continuo* from a manuscript in the Royal College of Music London: ed J A Parkinson (OUP). *Sonata in E major for 2 flutes and continuo* (CB

86

165): unpublished. *Sonata in D major for flute, guitar and viola da gamba*: ed Zanoskar (Sikorski, Hamburg), doubtful.

II.3 KEYBOARD MUSIC

II.3 (a) Suites: Harpsichord music, in 4 ' Collections ' (CB 58, 77, 95, 61).

Suites de pièces pour le clavecin: collection 1, suites 1-8; collection 2, suites 9-16; collection 3, leçons, etc; collection 4, fugues, etc.

Complete: HG 2; in LPS no 86; ed W Serauky and (for vol 4) F von Glasenapp (Mitteldeutscher Verlag, Halle); ed A Ruthardt (PH); ed G Ropartz (Durand, Paris).

Separately: collection 1; HHA ser IV 1 (' The eight grand suites '); ed R Steglich (Bä). This was rather severely criticised for its neglect of the manuscript sources, but it is still a good clean edition; also ed (Br); ed Galliard / Augener).

II.3 (b) Miscellaneous keyboard pieces, not necessarily included in HG

(CB 11) *3 Suites for harpsichord;* ed W Danckert in *Unbekannte Meisterwerken der Klaviermusik* (Bä). Not in HG.

(CB 172) *Klavierbuch aus der Jugendzeit*: HG 48; also ed Serauky (PH).

(CB 174) *Pieces for harpsichord* (from the Aylesford manuscripts in the Royal Music Library in the British Museum): ed W Barclay Squire and J A Fuller-Maitland, 2 vols (Schott). Not in HG, but one of the most delightful collections of all Handel's keyboard pieces, including some for two-manual harpsichord; several of the pieces are keyboard versions of orchestral works. Full list in CB. Pieces for harpsichord ' Cembalodarabok ': ed F Brodszky, from a manuscript in the National Library in Budapest (Zenemukiado Vallalat, Budapest). Authenticity very doubtful. Not in HG or CB.

(CB 169) *12 Fantasien und 4 Stücke für Cembalo*: a miscellaneous collection of pieces, mostly from Handel's early years; the majority are not in HG (Hug, Zurich).

The Babell arrangements: in 1717 the English composer and harpsichordist W Babell published a book of harpsichord pieces under the title of *Suites of the most celebrated lessons collected and*

87

fitted to the harpsichord or spinnet. These contain several items from Handel's *Rinaldo,* as well as pieces adapted from other composers, arranged as harpsichord lessons, presumably by Babell, yet at the same time possibly representing the kind of thing which Handel may have actually played in the theatre as *maestro al cembalo.* Chrysander reprinted the Handelian items, with one or two other harpsichord arrangements, in HG 48. They are of considerable interest, but how far they represent what Handel actually played or what Babell himself invented is difficult to say.

Duets

(CB 170) *2 Fugen in C* (Heinrichshofen, Wilhelmshaven). Spurious; actually by J Marsh.

(CB 172, no 3) *Suite à deux clavecins,* in C minor: all that is preserved of this work is the harpsichord 1 part, but the harpsichord 2 part has been very cleverly restored by Thurston Dart, thus making a delightful suite for two instruments (OUP).

Organ music (*see also* Organ Concertos, page 8)

(CB 61) *6 Fugues:* these are essentially the same as collection of the HG 2 vol. Modern eds by D Hellmann (PH) and by G Philips (PH). *4 Voluntaries*: ed F Routh (PH)—of somewhat doubtful authenticity. Not in HG.

Miscellaneous works of keyboard type

(CB 168) *Pastorale et thème avec variations pour harpe ou piano*: ed H J Zingel (Schott). This odd work was first published by Artaria in Vienna in 1826. Authenticity doubtful. Not in HG.

II.4 Miscellaneous
Clock Music

These delightful pieces, including the one charmingly named 'A voluntary or a flight of angels ', were written for Charles Clay's musical clock. They are not in HG. The sole source is in two of the Aylesford manuscripts now in the British Museum. The pieces were first brought to notice by W Barclay Squire in an article in *The musical quarterly* (1919, vol 15), in which he printed all of them.

The original instrument is described by Edward Croft-Murray in an article in *Country life* (31 Dec 1948), 'The ingenious Mr Clay'. Some modern editions are: suite for a musical clock, arr for organ by R Purvis (Flammer, NY); ten tunes for a musical clock, arr for organ by J R Lawson (Independent Music Publishers, NY); four pieces for a musical clock, arr for pf or organ by F Spiegl (Schott); also by Spiegl, for four recorders (Schott): sonata for a musical clock, arr for pf by C Clarke (Chappell).

Selected recordings of Handel's music

COMPILED BY BRIAN REDFERN

Handel has not yet received the attention from the recording companies which his music merits. The result is that the single recording which is listed under many works in the discography is often the only one currently available. Fortunately most of the items included are of a very high standard, and between them provide examples from most periods of Handel's life in most of the forms he used.

The arrangement of the discography follows closely that used by Charles Cudworth in the section on editions, with obvious omissions when no recording of a work is currently available. In order to avoid consultation of secondary lists and indexes I have tried to make the abbreviations of orchestral and other names self explanatory. Performers are cited as appropriate in the order: soloists, choir, orchestra, conductor.

When a recording included in the list has been deleted, it may be possible to borrow it from one of the many public gramophone libraries in both the United Kingdom and the United States. Quite often a full-price recording reappears on a cheaper label after its deletion at the higher price.

Any second catalogue number given is American. If there is no second number the recording may not be available in America except by import. American readers are referred to the excellent Schwann catalogue for prices and for a complete listing of American recordings, which include many only available in the United States, and which I have therefore not been able to hear. For British issues I have indicated the cheaper labels as follows * £1 to £2; † under £1.

Vocal music
OPERAS AND PASTICCIOS
As there are so few complete recordings of the operas I have included some recordings of recitals and concerts which contain individual items from several operas.

a) RECORDINGS OF SEPARATE OPERAS

Alcina:

Sutherland, Berganza, Freni, Sciutti, Sinclair, Alva, Flagello; London Sym Chorus & Orch; Bonynge. *GOS 509/11; London 1361 (3 recs), excerpts London 25874.

Giulio Cesare:

Sills, Forrester, Wolff, Treigle, Malas; NY City Opera Chorus & Orch; Redel. SER 5561/3; LSC 6182 (3 recs), excerpts LSC 3116.

(Excerpts) Elkins, Sinclair, Sutherland, Home, Conrad; New Sym Orch; Bonynge. *SDD 213; London 25876.

Sosarme:

Ritchie, Evans, Watts, Deller, Herbert, Kentish, Wallace; St Anthony Singers; St Cecilia Orch; Lewis. OL 50091/3.

b) SELECTIONS FROM SEVERAL OPERAS

Admeto: 'Cangio d'aspetto', Alcina: 'Verdi prati', Atalanta: 'Care selve'. Ottone: 'Vieni o figlio' 'La speranza', Partenope: 'Voglio dire', Rinaldo: 'Lascia ch'io panga', Rodelinda: 'Dove sei':

Greevy; Academy of St Martin in the Fields; Leppard. *Handel recital.* ZRG 501; Argo 5459.

Giulio Cesare: 'E pur cosi in un giorno' 'Piangero la sorte mia', Ottone: 'Vinto è l'amor', Rodelinda: 'Ombre, piante, urne funesti' 'Ho perduto', Serse: 'Un cenno leggiadretto':

Popp; Ambrosian Singers; English Chamber Orch; Fischer. *Recital.* ASD 2334.

Berenice: 'Si tra i ceppi', Floridante: 'Alma mia', Radamisto: 'Perfido! di a quell'empio tiranno', Rodelinda: 'Scacciata del suo nido', Tolomeo: 'Che piu si tarda omai' 'Stille amare':

Souzay; English Chamber Orch; Leppard. *Recital* SAL 3468.

Alcina: 'Tiranna gelosia' 'Torrami a vagheggiar' 'Ah! mio cor!', Giulio Cesare: 'Da tempeste il legno infranto' 'V'adoro pupille' 'Piangero la sorte mia':

Sutherland; London Sym; New Sym Orch of London; Covent Garden Orch; Bonynge, Boult, Molinari-Pradelli. *Handel recital.* SXL 6191.

Alcina: ' Pensa a chi geme ', Berenice: ' Si, tra i ceppi ', Ezio: ' Se un bell'ardire ':

Robinson; Academy of St Martin in the Fields; Ledger. *Handel recital.* ZRG 504.

c) OVERTURES, SUITES, ETC

Ariodante: Overture, Berenice: Overture, Rinaldo: Overture, march & battle, Teseo: Overture:

English Chamber Orch; Bonynge. *Handel concert.* SXL 6360; London 6586.

Arminio: Overture, Deidamia: Overture, Faramondo: Overture, Giulio Cesare: Overture and minuet from act 1, Radamisto: Overture, Scipio (Scipione): Overture:

English Chamber Orch; Bonynge. *Handel concert.* SXL 6496.

Rodrigo: Suite, Serse: Suite:

Lewis; Hallé Orch; Barbirolli. *Handel concert.* *GSGC 14086.

ORATORIOS, MASQUES, SERENADES, ODES

Acis and Galatea:

Sutherland, Pears, Galliver, Brannigan; St Anthony Singers; Philomusica of London; Boult. *SOL 60011/2; Oiseau Lyre 60011/2.

Alexander Balus:

Ritter, Fahberg, Gilvan, Hudermann, Hoberg; Mannheim Handel Choir; Hamburg Convivium Musicum Chamber Orch; Treiber MUS 30/2.

L'Allegro, il Penseroso ed il Moderato:

Morison, Harwood, Watts, Pears, Delman, Alan; Dart; Philomusica; Willcocks (does not include *Il Moderato*). *SOL 60025/6; Oiseau Lyre 60025/6.

Hercules:

Stich-Randall, Lerer, Forrester, Young, Quilico, Grabowski, Eder; Vienna Academy Chorus; Vienna Radio Orch; Priestman. SER 5569/71; LSC 6181 (3 recs).

Israel in Egypt:

Harper, Clark, Esswood, Young, Rippon, Keyte; Leeds Festival Chorus; English Chamber Orch; MacKerras. 2708020 (2 recs).

Burton, Allen, Chabay; Dessoff Choirs; Symphony of the Air; Boepple. †TV 37013/4S; SVUX 52019 (2 recs).

Jephtha:

Grist, Watts, Forrester, Woolf, Young, Lawrenson; Amor Artis Chorus; English Chamber Orch; Somary. C 10077/9; 6734001 (3 recs).

Messiah:

Harper, Watts, Wakefield, Shirley-Quirk; Aldis Singers; SAL 3584/6, excerpts SAL 3623; PHS-3-992 (3 recs), excerpts Philips 900214.

Harwood, Baker, Esswood, Tear, Herincx; Ambrosian Singers; English Chamber Orch; MacKerras. *HQS 1052/4, excerpts *HQS 1183; Angel S 3705 (3 recs), excerpts Angel S 36530.

Sutherland, Bumbry, McKellar, Ward; London Sym Chorus & Orch; Boult. SET 218/20, excerpts SXL 6009, SXL 6010; London 1329 (3 recs), excerpts London 25703, 25711, 25712.

Vyvyan, Sinclair, Vickers, Tozzi; Royal Phil Chorus & Orch; Beecham. SER 4501/4; LDS 6409 (4 recs), excerpts LDS 2447.

Schwarzkopf, Hoffman, Gedda, Hines; Phil Chorus & Orch; Klemperer. SAN 146/8; Angel S 3657 (3 recs), excerpts Angel 7 36324.

Harper, Watts, Robertson, Stalman; London Phil Chorus & Orch; Jackson. †STXID 5111/3, excerpts †STXID 15150.

Ode for St Cecilia's Day:

Cantelo, Partridge; King's College Choir, Cambridge; Academy of St Martin in the Fields; Willcocks. ZRG 563; Argo S 563.

Semele:

Griffith, Vyvyan, Watts, Whitworth, Herbert, James; St Anthony Singers; New Sym Orch; Lewis. †OLS 111/3.

Solomon:

Endich, Brooks, Young, Shirley-Quirk, Wolff; Vienna Volksoper; Simon. SER 5579/81; LSC 6187 (3 recs).

Marshall, Morison, Young, Cameron; Beecham Choral Society; Royal Phil; Beecham. *Arranged by Beecham.* *SCM 82/3; Seraphim S 6039 (2 recs).

Theodora:

Harper, Forrester, Lehane, Young, Fleet, Lawrenson; Amor Artis Chorale; English Chamber Orch; Somary. VXS 15000 (3 recs), C 10050/2.

ORCHESTRAL MUSIC FROM ORATORIOS, ETC

Alceste: grand entrée, Hercules: march, Samson: minuet. Forest music, Semele: Where'er you walk, Solomon: Sinfonia act 3. Entrance of the Queen of Sheba, Triumph of time and truth: sonata:
Biggs (organ); Royal Phil; Groves. *61230.

SECULAR MUSIC FOR VOICES
ITALIAN CANTATAS WITH INSTRUMENTS
Apollo e Dafne:

Ritchie, Boyce; Oiseau-Lyre Ensemble; Lewis. OL 50038.
Ah! crudel nel pianto mio, Armida abbandonata:
Baker; English Chamber Orch; Leppard. ASD 2468; Angel S 36569.
Carco sempre di Gloria, Splenda l'alba in Oriente, Tu fedel? tu costante:
Watts; English Chamber Orch; Leppard. *SOL 60046; Oiseau-Lyre 60046.
Crudel tiranno amor:
Ameling; English Chamber Orch; Leppard. *Handel recital.* 6500 008.

ITALIAN DUETS AND TRIOS
Se tu non lasci amore; Quel fior che all'alba ride; Cui nei Tartarei regni; Tacete, ohime, tacete; No, di voi non vo'fidarmi; ahi nelle sorti umane:
Sheppard, Le Sage, Bevan; Elliott (harpsichord); Ryan (gamba). †ORYX 704.

CANTATAS WITH WORDS IN ENGLISH
Look down harmonious saint:
Tear; Academy of St Martin in the Fields; Marriner. *Recital.* ZRG 661.

9 Deutsche Arien:
 Speiser; Winterthur Baroque Quintet. †TV 34024S.

LATIN MOTETS, PSALMS, ETC
Dixit Dominus:
 Zylis-Gara, Baker, Lane, Tear, Shirley-Quirk; King's College Choir; English Chamber Orch; Willcocks. ASD 2262; Angel S 36331.
Dixit Dominus:
 Donath, Koeleman, Heynis, Dolder, Hollestelle; NLRV Vocal Ensemble; Amsterdam Chamber Orch; Voorberg. 6500 044.
Silete venti:
 Lukomska; Collegium Aureum; Reinhardt. *With* Overture to Joseph. OHM 636.
 Ameling; English Chamber Orch; Leppard. *Handel recital.* 6500 008.

ENGLISH ANTHEMS AND PSALMS
CHANDOS ANTHEMS
(6) As pants the hart, (10) The Lord is my light:
 Cantelo, Partridge, King's College Choir; Academy of St Martin in the Fields; Davis (organ); Willcocks. ZRG 541; ZRG 541.
(9) O praise the Lord with one consent, (11) Let God arise:
 Vaughan, Young, Robinson; King's College Choir; Academy of St Martin in the Fields; Willcocks. ZRG 5490; Argo 5490.

CORONATION ANTHEMS
Zadok the Priest, The King shall rejoice, My heart is inditing, Let thy hand be strengthened:
 King's College Choir; English Chamber Orch; Willcocks. ZRG 5369; Argo 5369.
 Ambrosian Singers; Menuhin Festival Orch; Menuhin. ASD 2584; Angel S 36741.

ENGLISH LITURGICAL MUSIC
Utrecht Te Deum and *Jubilate:*
 Wolfe, Watts, Brown, Fleet, Hemsley; Geraint Jones Singers &

Orch; Jones. *With* Coronation anthem: Zadok the Priest.   198008;
198008.

Instrumental music

ORCHESTRAL

Oboe concertos nos 1 B flat major, 2 B flat major, 3 G minor:

Goosens; Bath Festival Orch; Menuhin. *Concert*   ASD 500;
Angel S 36103.

Lord; Academy of St Martin in the Fields; Marriner. *Handel concert.*   ZRG 5442;   Argo 5442.

Oboe concerto no 3 G minor:

Pierlot; Jean-François Paillard Ensemble; Paillard. *Handel concert.*   *ST 270.

Casier; Cento Soli Orch; Bernard. *With* concerti grossi op 3 nos
2, 4, 5,   *H 71013;   Nonesuch 71013.

Concerti grossi op 3:

Academy of St Martin in the Fields; Marriner.   ZRG 5400;
Argo 5400.

Mainz Chamber Orch; Kehr.   †TV 34103S;   Turnabout 34103.
Boyd Neel Orch; Neel.   †ECS 509.

Concerti grossi op 3 nos 2 B flat major, 4 F major, 5 D minor:

Cento Soli Orch; Bernard. *With* oboe concerto.   *H 71013;
Nonesuch 71013.

Concerti grossi op 6:

Academy of St Martin in the Fields; Marriner.   SXL 6369/71;
London 2309 (3 recs).

English Chamber Orch; Leppard.   6703003 (3 recs);   SR-3-9124
(3 recs).

Schola Cantorum Basiliensis; Wenzinger.   2710 003 (3 recs);
2710 003 (3 recs).

Concerti grossi op 6 nos 1 G major, 2 F major, 4 A major, 5 D major:

Bath Festival Orch; Menuhin.   †ST 1043;   Angel S 3647 (op 6
complete 4 recs).

Concerti grossi op 6 nos 3 E minor, 6 G minor, 10 D minor, 12 B minor:

Bath Festival Orch; Menuhin. *ST 944;   Angel S 3647 (op 6 complete 4 recs).
Concerti grossi op 6 nos 7 B flat major, 8 C minor, 9 F major, 11 A major:
Bath Festival Chamber Orch; Menuhin.   *ST 817;   Angel S 3647 (op 6 complete 4 recs).
Concerto grosso C major 'Alexander's Feast':
Philomusica of London; Jones. *Handel concert.* *SOL 60013; Oiseau-Lyre 60013.
Capella Coloniensis, Schola Cantorum Basiliensis; Wenzinger. *Handel concert.* 198392;   2708003.

ORGAN CONCERTOS

Op 4 nos 1 G minor, 2 B flat major, 3 G minor, 4 F major:
Richter; Chamber Orch.   SXL 2115.
Op 4 nos 5 F major, 6 B flat major, op 7 nos 1 B flat major, 2 A major:
Richter; Chamber Orch.   SXL 2187.
Op 7 nos 3 B flat major, 4 D minor, 5 G minor, 6 B flat major:
Richter; Chamber Orch.   SXL 2201.
Op 4 nos 1 G minor, 2 B flat major, 3 G minor:
Müller; Schola Cantorum Basiliensis; Wenzinger. *With* harp concerto.   198410;   2723005 (organ concertos complete 5 recs).
Op 4 no 4 F major, op 7 nos 2 G minor, 5 G minor, Seiffert no 13 F major:
Müller; Choir; Schola Cantorum Basiliensis; Wenzinger.   198393; 2723005 (organ concertos complete 5 recs).
Op 4 nos 1 G minor, 5 F major, Seiffert nos 13 F major, 14 A major:
Preston; Bath Festival Orch; Menuhin.   ASD 2352.
Op 4 nos 2 B flat major, 3 G minor, op 7 no 3 B flat major, Seiffert no 15 D minor:
Preston; Menuhin Festival Orch; Menuhin.   ASD 2534;   Angel S 36700.
Op 4 nos 4 F major, 6 B flat major, op 7 nos 2 A major, 4 D minor:
Preston; Menuhin Orch; Menuhin.   ASD 2443.
Op 7 nos 1 B flat major, 5 G minor, 6 B flat major:
Preston; Menuhin Festival Orch; Menuhin.   ASD 2662.

Op 4 nos 1 G minor, 2 B flat major, 4 F major, op 7 no 1 B flat major:
Downes; London Chamber Orch; Bernard. RC 736; Music Guild S 102.
Op 4 nos 1 G minor, 4 F major, Seiffert no 13 F major:
Dallman; Heidelberg Chamber Orch. †EXP 33.
Op 4 no 4 F major, op 7 no 2 A major:
Klerk; Amsterdam Chamber Orch; Horst. *With* concerto grosso op 6 no 6. SAWT 9437; Telefunken S 9437.
Seiffert nos 14 A major, 15 D minor, 16 F major:
Klerk; Amsterdam Chamber Orch; Horst. SAWT 9441; Telefunken S 9441.
Op 4 no 5 F major (as Harp concerto):
Ellis; Philomusica of London; Jones. *Handel concert.* *SOL 60013; Oiseau-Lyre 60013.
Op 4 no 6 B flat major (as Harp concerto):
Zingel; Schola Cantorum Basiliensis; Wenzinger. *With* organ concertos op 4 nos 1-4.
Zabaleta; Paul Kuentz Chamber Orch; Kuentz. *Concert.* 139304; DGG 139304.
Korchinska; London Baroque Ensemble; Haas. *Concert.* *GGC 4043; Vanguard S 199.
Op 4 no 6 B flat major (as lute and harp concerto):
Dupré; Ellis; Philomusica of London; Jones. *Handel concert.* *SOL 60013; Oiseau-Lyre 60013.

OCCASIONAL MUSIC
Water music (arr Boyling):
Bath Festival Orch; Menuhin. ASD 577; Angel S 36173.
Water music suite:
Berlin Phil; Kubelik. *With* Fireworks music. 138864; DGG 138864.
Water music suite (arr Harty):
Royal Phil; Weldon. *With* Fireworks music suite (arr Harty) *SXLP 20033.
London Phil; Beinum. *With* Fireworks music suite (arr Harty) *ACL 162.
Royal Phil; Sargent. *Handel concert.* ASD 286.

Water music suite (arr Harty & Szell):
London Sym; Szell. *Handel concert.* *SDD 169; London 6236.
Fireworks music:
Berlin Phil; Kubelik. *With* Water music suite. 138864; DGG 138864.

Jean-François Paillard Ensemble; Paillard. *Handel concert.* *ST 270.

Pro Arte Orch; MacKerras. *With* double concerto no 2 F major. *GSGC 14003; Vanguard S 289.

Menuhin Festival Orch; Menuhin. *Handel concert.* ASD 2485; Angel S 36604.
Fireworks music suite (arr Harty):
Royal Phil; Weldon. *With* Water music suite (arr Harty). *SXLP 20033.

London Phil; Beinum. *With* Water music suite (arr Harty). *ACL 152.

London Sym; Szell. *Handel concert.* *SDD 169; London 6236.
Royal Phil; Sargent. *Handel concert.* ASD 286.

MISCELLANEOUS ORCHESTRAL WORKS
Double concertos no 1 B flat major, no 2 F major, no 3 F major:
English Chamber Orch; Leppard. SAL 3707.
Double concerto no 1 B flat major:
Jean-François Paillard Ensemble; Paillard. *Handel concert.* *ST 270.

Menuhin Festival Orch; Menuhin. *Handel concert.* ASD 2485; Angel S 36604.
Double concerto no 2 F major:
Pro Arte Orch; MacKerras. *With* Fireworks music. *GSGC 14003; Vanguard S 289.
Double concerto no 3 F major:
Capella coloniensis; Schola Cantorum Basiliensis; Wenzinger. *Handel concert.* 198392.
Violin concerto B flat major:
Menuhin Festival Orch; Menuhin. *Handel concert.* ASD 2485; Angel S 36604.
The gods go a'begging, Amaryllis gavotte and scherzo, Arrival of the

Queen of Sheba (all arranged Beecham):
Royal Phil; Beecham. *Concert.* *ST 837.
Love in Bath (arr Beecham):
Hollweg; Royal Phil; Beecham. *ST 632; Seraphim S 60039.

Chamber music

SOLO SONATAS WITH CONTINUO

Sonatas for violin and continuo op 1 nos 3, 10, 12, 13, 14, 15:
Menuhin (violin); Gauntlett (gamba); Malcolm (harpsichord)
ASD 2384.
Grumiaux (violin); Veyron-Lacroix (harpsichord). SAL 3687.
*Sonatas for violin and continuo op 1 nos 1 b, 3, 6, 10, 12, 13, 14,
15, and in G major, A major:*
Melkus (violin); Wenzinger (cello); Scheidt (lute); Müller (harpsi-
chord). 198474/5; 2708014 (2 recs).
Sonatas for flute and continuo op 1 nos 1, 2, 4, 5:
Bennett (flute); Nesbitt (gamba); Lester (harpsichord). †RCB 3.
*Sonatas for recorder and continuo op 1 nos 2, 4, 7, 11 and in B flat
major, D minor:*
Brüggen (recorder); Bylsma (cello); Leonhardt (harpsichord).
SAWT 542; Telefunken S 9421.
Sonatas for recorder and continuo op 1 nos 2, 4, 7, 11:
Linde (recorder); Wenzinger (gamba); Leonhardt (harpsichord).
SOHM 617; VICS 1429.
Sonatas for oboe and continuo op 1 nos 6, 8 and in B flat major:
Holliger (oboe); Cervera (cello); Picht-Axenfeld (harpsichord).
SAL 3772.
Trio sonata op 5 no 2:
Goldsborough Ensemble. *Recital.* *SOL 319.

KEYBOARD MUSIC

Harpsichord suites nos 1-4:
Dart. †OL 50184.
Harpsichord suites nos 1, 5, 7, 8:
Heiller. *VSL 11009.
Harpsichord suites nos 2, 3, 4, 6:
Heiller. *VSL 11008.

Chaconne and 21 variations G major, Fantasia C major, Minuet G minor, Prelude, air and 5 variations B flat major:
Malcolm. *Recital.* *HQS 1085.
Voluntary C major, Fugue A minor, Cornet voluntary G minor, Fugue C minor (all on the organ): Suite E major, Fantasy C major, Fugue A minor, Fugue C minor (all on the harpsichord): Suite C minor for 2 harpsichords:
Jackson (organ, harpsichord), Barker (harpsichord). *With* Hunting song, Pigeon's air (Langridge, tenor). †ORYX 1718.

CLOCK MUSIC
5 pieces for Clay's musical clock:
Haselboeck (organ). †ORYX 1759.

GUITAR ARRANGEMENTS
Sarabande and variations, Minuets 1 and 2, Fughetto. Gavotte:
Ragossnig (guitar). STU 70647.

Index

No entries are included for the recordings of Handel's music.

Aaron, H 69

Abraham, G (*ed*) *Handel: a symposium* 51, 57; on Handel's style 51

Académie Royale de Musique in Paris 20

Account of the musical performances in Westminster Abbey (Burney) 45

Account of the visit of Handel to Dublin (Townsend) 52

Aci, Galatea e Polifemo composed and performed in Naples 12

Acis and Galatea 12; performed at Canons 19; in London 24

'*Acis and Galatea* in the eighteenth century ' (Smith) 52

Acta musicologica 50

Addison, J 16

Adler, S 78

Admeto performed in London 23

Admetus see Admeto

Aetius see Ezio

Agrippina performed in Venice 12

Aix-la-Chapelle 28; Peace of 37

Alceste composition of 38

Alcina performed in London 27

Alessandro performed in London 23

Alessandro in India (Metastasio) 24

Alessandro Severo performed in London 28

Alexander, operas on, see *Alessandro*

Alexander Balus performed in London 37

Alexander's feast performed in London 27, 28

Allegro, il penseroso ed il moderato performed in London 29; in Dublin 32, 33

Almira performed in Hamburg 11

Alvito, Duke of 12

Amadigi performed in London 17

Amadis see Amadigi

Amaryllis suite (Handel-Beecham) 85

Ameln, K 65, 71

Anecdotes of G F Handel and J C Smith (Anon) 46

Anne, Princess, marriage of 26

Anne, Queen 14, 16

Arbuthnot, J 16, 18

Arcadian societies in Italy 13

Archer, J S 75, 83

Arianna, performed in London 26

Ariadne see Arianna

Ariodante performed in London 27

Ariosti, A 23

Arminio performed in London 27

Arminius see Arminio

Arnold, S 59; *Prodigal son* 35

Artillery drums, the 52

Atalanta performed in London 27

Athaliah performed in Oxford 26, 27

Attilio *see* Ariosti, A

Augustus, Duke of Saxe-Magdeburg 7

Avolio or Avoglio, Signora 32
Aylesford mss 87, 88

Babell, W 87, 88
Bach, J S Brandenburg concertos of 30; comparisons with Handel 42, 43, 52, 53, 55
Bach and Handel; the consummation of the Baroque in music (Davison) 53
Baines, A 82, 83
Bairstow, E C *Handel's oratorio the Messiah* 54
Bantock, Sir G 69, 70, 71, 82, 83
Barnby, Sir J 71, 79
Barrett Lennard collection, the 58
Beard, J 27
Bee, The 25
Beecham, Sir T 84, 85
Beethoven, L van 43
Beggar's opera performed in London 19, 24
Bell, A Craig *Handel: a chronological list of his works* 57
Belshazzar performed in London 36
Bennett, W S 60
Benson, A J *Handel's Messiah; the oratorio and its history* 53
Bergmann, W 75, 84
Berlin, Handel in 9
Berlioz, H on Handel 47
Best, T M G 66
Best, W T 73
Biggs, E P 82
Binitz, von 11
Bishop, J 74
Blom, E revision of C F A Williams' biography 48, 50; version of *Fireworks music* by 83
Böhm, G 77
Bolton, Duchess of 18
Bondreau, R A 83
Bonet on the *Water music* 17, 18
Bononcini or Buononcini, G 21, 31
Bonnie Prince Charlie, *see* Stuart, Prince C E
Bordoni, F 23
Bornefeld, H 72
Borrowings, Handel's *see* plagiarism
Boschi, G M 22
Boult, Sir A 70
Bourne, T W 73

Bower, Sir J D 81
Boyce, W 31, 42, 48
Brahms, J 76
Brian, H 76
Brissler, F 71, 72
Britton, T 14
Brodsley, F 87
Brown, J 74
Brückner-Ruggeberg, W 72
Bryan, G 74
Brydges, J Earl of Carnarvon and Duke of Chandos 18, 19, 49
Burlington, Earl of 16
Burney, C 31, 32, 59; *An account of the musical performances in Westminster Abbey* 45, 59
Butler, S 47
Buxtehude, D 10
Byrom, J 21

Canons or Cannons 18, 19, 20
Cantatas, Handel's, J Herbage on 51
Cantatas, Handel's Italian 12
Carestini, G 26
Carse, A 72
Carissimi, G 34
Carnarvon, Earl of *see* Brydges, J
Caroline, Queen 28
Casadesus, H 84
Catalogue of the music in the Fitzwilliam Museum, Cambridge (Fuller-Maitland and Mann) 58
Catalogues of Handel exhibitions 55
Catalogues of Handel's works 51, 57
Central Music Library, London 67
Chamber music, Handel's, J Horton on 51
Chandos anthems 18, 19
Chandos, Duke of *see* Brydges, J
Charles Edward Stuart *see* Stuart, Prince C E
Chester, Handel in 31, 32
Choice of Hercules performed in London 39
Chronological catalogue of Handel's works (A Craig Bell) 57
Chrysander, F *G F Händel* 46, 47; proposed catalogue of Handel's works 57; various editions by 60-65, 73, 74, 89
Church music, Handel's, E Blom on 51

Clark, R *On the sacred oratorio of the Messiah* 46; *Reminiscences of Handel* etc 46
Clarke, C 89
Clay, C 88, 89
Clutsam, G H 83
Coleman, H 74
Collins, A 69, 70
Colonna family, the 12
Colyns, J B 85
Commemorative exhibition of the 250th anniversary of the births of G F Handel and J S Bach (Fitz-william Museum, Cambridge) 55
Concerning Handel (Smith) 52
Concerti a due cori 43
Concerti grossi, op 3 composition and publication of 26; of op 6 29
Concertos, organ, op 4, F etc 26, 28, 39, 81
Congreve, W 36
Coopersmith, J 57, 60; *Messiah* ed by 74
Coram, T 38
Corelli, A 12, 13, 30
Coronation anthems for George II 23, 24
Correspondence, Handel's *see* Letters
Country life 89
Covent Garden theatre, Handel's connection with 26
Cowen, F W 71
Coxe, W supposed author of the *Anecdotes of Handel,* etc 46
Cranmer, P 71
Craxton, H 80
Croft-Murray, E 89
Crotch, W 48
Cudworth, C L 83
Culwick, J C *Handel's Messiah· discovery of the original word-book . . .* 53
Cumberland, Duke of 37, 38
Cummings, W H 48, 75
Cuzzoni, F 22

Dale, K on Handel's keyboard music 51
Danckert, W 71, 86, 87
Darlow, D 77
Dart, R T 80, 86, 88
Dart, T *see* Dart, R T

Davison, A T *Bach and Handel; the consummation of the Baroque in music* 53
Deal and Walmer Handelian Society 50
Dean, W *Handel and the opera seria* 55; *Handel's dramatic ora-torios and masques* 53; ' Handel's dramatic works ' 56
Deborah performed in London 25; in Oxford 26
Deidamia performed in London 29
Dent, E J 31, 51; *Handel* 50; on Handel's operas 51
Dettingen, battle of 36
Dettingen Te deum see *Te deum, Dettingen*
Deutsch, O E 45, 77; *Handel, a documentary biography* 44; *Selection from the original manuscript of the Messiah* 73
Deutsche Arien, Handel's 9
Deutsche Händel-Gesellschaft 44, 60
Dixit dominus, composition and date of 12
Dörffel, A 72
Dolmetsch, A 86
Dresden, Handel in 17; Hasse at 23
Drums, Handel's 52
Dryden, J 29; *Alexander's feast* by 27; *Ode on St Cecilia's day* 29
Dublin, Handel in 32-34, 52
Dublin journal, Faulkner's 33, 34
Dubourg, M 32
Duck, L 58, 82, 83
Dunn, G 75
Dupré, M 81, 82
Durastanti, M 22
Dusseldorf 13, 15; Elector of 13

' Earliest editions of Messiah ' (Smith) 52; of ' Water music ' (Smith) 52
Early English musical magazine 77
Early moral criticism of Handelian oratorio (Myers) 53
Easdale, B 75
Edgware, Handel's connection with 19, 20
Edinburgh Festival of 1948, Handel exhibition at 55, 56
Edmundson, H 74
Edwards, F G 74

Elgar, Sir E 79
England, Handel's first visit to 13, 14; second, etc 15
Erba, D 48
Esther performed in London 24, 26; in Oxford 28; see also *Haman and Mordecai*
Ewerhart, R 78
Exhibition catalogues, various 55
Ezio performed in London 25

Faithful shepherd see *Pastor fido*
Faithful shepherd suite (Handel-Beecham) 85
Faramondo, performed in London 28
Farinelli (*ie* Broschi, C) 16
Farmer, H G *Handel's kettledrums* 52
Faulkner's Dublin journal see *Dublin journal*
Fellerer, K G 65
Fiebeg, K 78
' Finance and patronage in Handel's life ' (Smith) 52
Finances, Handel's 52
Fireworks Music see *Music for the Royal Fireworks*
Fitzwilliam Museum, Cambridge 55; Handel mss in 58
Flavio performed in London 22
Flesch, S 66, 70, 86
Floridante, performed in London 22
Flower, Sir N 49, 52, 58; *George Frideric Handel* 49, 50
Forbes, W 86
Fortune, N *Purcell-Handel Festival, London, June 1959* 56
Foundling Hospital, London 38
Franz, R 73
Frederick, Prince of Wales 35, 37; *Wedding anthem* for 27
Frotscher, G 70
Fuchs, J N 69
Fuller-Maitland, J A and Mann, A H *Catalogue of the music in the Fitzwilliam Museum* 87
Funeral anthem (*The ways of Zion*) 28
Furth, K J 69

Gates, B 24
Gay, J 16, 19, 24

George I, King of England 17, 23
George II, King of England, 23, 36
George Frideric Handel (Flower) 49; (Lang) 51; (Rackwitz and Stefan) 50
Gerber, R 71
German Handel Society see *Deutsche Händel-Gesellschaft*
Gerusalemme liberata (Tasso) 14
Gervinus, G 70, 75
Gevaert, F A 85
Giesler, W 70
Giulio Cesare performed in London 23
Giustino performed in London 27
Glasenapp, F von 87
Gluck, C W von 36
Godolphin, Countess 41
Gods go a-begging suite (Handel-Beecham) 85
Goethe, J W von 43
Goossens, L 80
Grand concertos, op 6 see *concerti grossi, op 6*
Granville, B 40
Great elopement suite (Handel-Beecham) 85
Grove, Sir G *Dictionary of music and musicians*, 5th ed 52, 57
' Gustavus Waltz : was he Handel's cook?' (Smith) 52

Haas, K 84
Händel-Bibliographie (Sasse) 44
Händel-Jahrbuch 44, 66
Hall, J S *Handel* 50
Hall, J S and M V 65, 72
Halle, Handel's birthplace 7, 15, 17, 24, 58
Haman and Mordecai performed at Canons 24, 35; see also *Esther*
Hamburg, Handel in 10, 11, 17; Handel mss in 58
Hamilton, N 30
Handel, Dorothea née Taust, Handel's mother 8, 15; Dorothea, Handel's elder sister 9,15; Georg senior, Handel's father, 8, 9; Johanna Christiana, Handel's younger sister 9, 15
Handel (Dent) 50
Handel (Hall) 50
Handel (Rolland) 49
Handel (Sadie) 51

Handel (Streatfeild) 49
Handel (Weinstock) 50
Handel (Young) 50
Handel. A descriptive catalogue of the early editions (Smith and Humphries) 58
Handel. A documentary biography (Deutsch) 44
Handel. A symposium (Abraham) 51
Handel and his autographs (King) 58
Handel and his orbit (Robinson) 48
' Handel and the English church ' (Lam) 56
Handel and the opera seria (Dean) 55
Handel at Canons (Sibley) 49
Handel at Vauxhall (Hodgkinson) 52
Handel at work (Tobin) 53
Handel autographs in the British Museum (Streatfield) 58
Handel, Canons and the Duke of Chandos (Streatfield) 49
Handel commemoration of 1784 59
Handel, Dryden and Milton (Myers) 53
Handel in England (Herbage) 56
Handel manuscripts vol I of *Catalogue of the King's music library* (Squire) 58
' Handel the man ' (Smith) 52
' Handel the man ' (Young) 51
Handel, His life and works (Williams) 48, 50
Handelian's notebook (Smith) 52
Handel's dramatic oratorios and masques (Dean) 56
' Handel's failure in 1747 ' (Smith) 52
' Handel's kettledrums ' (Farmer) 52
Handel's Messiah. Catalogue of an exhibition . . . (King) 56
Handel's Messiah. A critical account of the ms sources and printed editions (Tobin) 55
Handel's Messiah. Discovery of the original wordbook (Culwick) 53
Handel's Messiah. The oratorio and its history (Benson) 53
Handel's Messiah. Origins, composition, sources (Larsen) 54

Handel's Messiah. A touchstone of taste (Myers) 54
' Handel's musical instruments ' (Redlich) 56
Handel's oratorio the Messiah (Bairstow) 54
Hanover, George, Elector of 13, 15, 16; *see also* George I
Hanover, Handel in 13, 15, 17
Harmonious blacksmith, the 20, 46
Harty, Sir H 82, 83
Hasse, J A 23, 27
Hautboy concertos, *see* concerti grossi, op 3
Hawkins, Sir J *History of music* 15, 30
Haydn, F J 35
Haynes, B 78
Heidegger or Heidecker, J J 17, 20, 28
Hellmann, D 88
Henry Purcell . . . George Frideric Handel . . . Catalogue of a commemorative exhibition (King) 56
Henry Watson Library, Manchester 49, 50
Herbage, J 51, 70; *Handel in England* 56; the *Messiah* 54
Hercules, performed in London 36
Herrmann, W 79
Hicks, M 75
Hill, A 14
Hillemann, W 81, 86
Hinnenthal, J P 66, 84, 85
Hirsch, P 60
Hodgkinson, T *Handel at Vauxhall* 52
Hoffmann, A 66, 80, 84
Holschneider, A 71, 73, 74
Horton, J on Handel's chamber music 51
Hudson, F 66, 80
Hughes, J 76
Hull, A E 49
Humphreys, S 25
Humphries, C *see* Smith, W C and Humphries, C
Hunt, E 75
Hymen see *Imeneo*

Imeneo, performed in London 29
Indebtedness of Handel to other composers (Taylor) 48

'The ingenious Mr Clay ' 89
Ireland, Handel in *see* Dublin
Israel in Egypt, composition and performances of 28, 34, 35, 39; Mendelssohn's edition of 60
Italy, Handel in 11, 20, 24

Jacobsen, M 85, 86
Jacques, R 69, 70, 74
James, P 79
Janson 32
Jennens, C 28-32
Jephtha, composition and performance of 39
Johnson, S 16, 42
Jones, H F 47
Joseph and his brethren performed in London 36
Joshua performed in London 31; March in 37
Judas Maccabaeus performed in London 37
Julius Caesar see *Giulio Cesare*
Jupiter in Argos composition of 70
Justin see *Giustino*

Keiser, R 10
Keller, H 81
Keyboard music, K Dale on Handel's 51
Kickstat, P 69
Kielmanseg or Kielmanseck, Baron 17, 18; Mme de 18
King, A H catalogues of British Museum exhibitions by 56, 58; *Handel and his autographs* 58
Kingsbury, C 83
Kipnis, I 83
Kirkendale, U on the Ruspoli documents 12
Knapp, J M 49, 50
Kogel, K F 80
Kolneder, W 86
Kretschmar, H 74

Lam, B on Handel's church music 51; on the orchestral music 51
Lambert, C 81
Lamoureux, C 72
Lang, C S 70, 79, 81
Lang, P H *George Frideric Handel* 51

Lange, S de 81
Largo, Handel's see *Ombra mai fu*
Larsen, J P *Handel's Messiah; origins, composition, sources* 54
Latham, A G 70
Laudate pueri, date of 12
Lawson, J R 89
Lazell, L 71
Legh, C 77
Lehmann 69, 71
Leipzig 7
Letters, Handel's 45, 52
Letters and writings of G F Handel (Müller) 45
Lewis, A 71, 72, 75; on Handel's songs 51
Ley, H 69
Liedecke, H 82
Life of G F Handel (Rockstro) 47
Life of Handel (Schoelcher)
London Handel Society 60
London, Handel's arrival in 13ff; Italian opera in 16
Lotario performed in London 24
Lotharius, see *Lotario*
Lotti, A 31
Love in Bath (Handel-Beecham) 85
Lowe, J 47
Lucas, C 72
Ludwig, E 50
Lübeck, Handel's visit to 10
Lully, J B 20

MacKerras, C 83
Macfarren, Sir G 60, 72, 75
Macswiney or Macsweeny or Sweeny 15
Mainwaring, J *Memoirs of the life of the late G F Handel* 45
Mann, A 50, 73
Mann, A H 48, 77; *see also* Fuller-Maitland, J A and Mann, A H
March in *Joshua* 31; in *Scipio* 23
Marlborough, Duke of 18
Marsh, J 88
Mattei, F (' Pippo ') 21
Matthaei, K 66
Mattheson, J 10, 11, 17
Matthew, A G 74, 75
May, H 80
Medici, Prince F de 12
Memoirs of the life of the late G F Handel (Mainwaring) 45

Mendelssohn-Bartholdy, F 35, 60, 72
Mercer's Hospital, Dublin 34
Messiah, origins and compositions of 28, 30, 31; performances of, in Dublin 33, 34; in London 34-5, 38, 40; various editions of 73, 74; writings on 53, 54, 46; see also *Handel's Messiah*
Metastasio, P 24
Michaelson, D née Handel, Handel's elder sister 8, 15; Michaelson, M D, Handel's brother-in-law 15
Michelangelo and Handel 43
Miller, R B 71
Milton, J 29, 30, 35
Mirtillo suite 70
Moderato, 3rd part of *L'Allegro,* etc 29
Mohr, W 82
Monk, W H 72
Morell, T 37
Morgan, B O 70
Moscheles, I 60
Mottl, F 80
Moyse, L 86
Mozart, W A 71, 73, 74
Müller, E H *Letters and writings of G F Handel* 45
Müller, H 71
Müller-Hartmann, R 74
Muffat, Gottlieb 30, 31
Musick for the Royal Fireworks 37, 38, 43
Music in western civilisation (Lang) 51
Music review 60
Musical times 48
Muzio Scevola performed in London 21
Myers, R M *Early moral criticism of Handelian oratorio* 53; *Handel, Dryden and Milton* 53; *Handel's Messiah; a touchstone of taste* 54

Naples, Handel in 12
Naturalisation, Handel's 23
Neher, C 72
Nero produced in Hamburg 11
'New letters of the composer' (Smith) 52
Nisi dominus, date of 12

Northway, P 66
Novello, V 71-73

Occasional oratorio performed in London 37
Ode for the birthday of Queen Anne 15
Ode on St Cecilia's day 29
Ombra mai fu (Handel's ' Largo ') 28
On the sacred oratorio of the Messiah (Clark) 46
Opera of the Nobility 25
Opera seria 16, 55
Operas, Handel's E J Dent on 51, 55; W Dean on 55
Orange, the Prince of 26
Oratorios, Handel's 34, 51; W Dean on 53; P Young on 53
Orchestral music, Handel's, B Lam on 51
Orkney, Earl of 18
Orlando performed in London 25
Otho or *Otto* see *Ottone*
Ottoboni, Cardinal P 12
Ottone performed in London 22
Overtures, Handel's, as programme music 49
Oxford, Handel in 25, 26

Palmer, K 74
Paradise lost see Milton, J
Parkinson, J A 86
Parnasso in festa performed in London 26
Partenope performed in London 24
Pastor fido I performed in London 15; rewritten as *Pastor fido II* 26
Patronage in Handel's life, Smith on 52
Pearson, W D 71, 72
Pepusch, J C 19, 24
Phillips, G 82, 88
Pianto di Maria, performed in Italy 12
Pippo *see* Mattei
Pittman, J 82
Plagiarisms, Handel's 30, 31, 48
Platt, N 75
Pope, A 16
Poro performed in London 24
Porpora, N 25
Portraits of Handel, Smith on 52

Porus see *Poro*
Powell, W the 'Harmonious Black-
smith' 20, 46
'Present state of Handel research',
in 1969 (A Mann and J M Knapp)
50
Prout, E 72, 74, 75
Ptolemy see *Tolomeo*
Purcell-Handel Festival of 1959 56
Purcell, H influence of, on Handel
14, 56
Purvis, R 89

Rackwitz, W and Stefans, H
*George Frideric Handel: a bio-
graphy in pictures* 50
Radamisto performed in London
21
Radamistus see *Radamisto*
Rahlwes, A 74
Rawlinson, H 69, 71
Redlich, H F 66, 80, 82, 83; on
Handel's musical instruments 56
*Reminiscences of Handel, His
Grace the Duke of Chandos* etc
(Clark) 46
Rennart, G 72
Resurrezione, La 12, 13
Riccardo primo performed in Lon-
don 24
Rich, J 24, 26
Richard I see *Riccardo primo*
Rimbault, E F 60
Rinaldo, Handel's first London
opera 14, 17
Ripin, E M 83
Robinson, P *Handel and his orbit*
48
Rockstro, W S *Life of G F Handel*
47
Rodelinda performed in London 23
Rodemann, A 86
Roland see *Orlando*
Rolland, R *Handel* 49
Rome, Handel in 12
Ropartz, G 87
Rose, B 65, 75
Rossi, G 14
Roth, H 71, 75, 77, 80
Roubiliac, L F 41
Routh, F 88
Royal Academy of Music 20, 24
Royal Fireworks Music see *Musick
for the Royal Fireworks*

Ruckert, H 69
Ruspoli documents 11, 12; Marquis
F M 11, 12
Ruthardt, A 81, 87

Sadie, S *Handel* 51
Sallé, M 26, 27
Salzedo, C 81
Samson composed immediately
after *Messiah* 30; performed in
London 34
Samson Agonistes see Milton, J
Sartorius, H A 83
Sasse, K *Händel-Bibliographie* 44
Saul performed in London 28
Saxe-Weissenfels, Duke of 7, 8
Scarlatti, A 13
Scarlatti, D 11, 12, 13
Scheidt, S 7
Schering, A 70, 72-74, 83
Schmidt *see* Smith J C, the elder
Schmitz, H P 66, 85
Schneider, M 65, 78
Schoelcher, V 47; *Life of Handel*
47
Schroeder, F 65, 77, 80
Schubert, F 45
Schumann, G 80
Schütz, H 34
Scipio see *Scipione*
Scipione performed in London 23
Seiffert, M 72, 73, 76, 78-86
*Selection from the original manu-
script of the Messiah* (Deutsch) 73
Semele, performed in London 36
Senesino, F B 16, 22, 25
Serauky, W 87
Serse performed in London 28
Servadoni, Signor 38
Shakespeare and Handel 43
Sharp, T 39
Shaw, G B 35
Shaw, H W 73, 74, 79; *A textual
and historical companion to Han-
del's Messiah* 54; *The story of
Handel's Messiah* 54
Sibley, J C *Handel at Canons* 49
Siegmund-Schultze, W 65, 66, 69,
72, 74
Siena, Handel in 12
Silas, E 79
Silla possibly performed in Bur-
lington House 16
Siroe performed in London 24

Sitt, H 85
Smart, Sir G 60
Smith, J C the elder and the younger 17, 45, 54, 58
Smith, W C 76 catalogues of Handel's works by 51, 57; bibliography by in Flower's *G F Handel* 50; *Concerning Handel* 52; *A Handelian's notebook* 52; Introduction to *Edinburgh Festival* Exhibition of 1948 56
Smith, W C and Humphries, C *Handel: a descriptive catalogue of the early editions* 58, 59
Smollett, T 38
Smyth, J 40
Soldan, K 73
Solomon performed in London 37
'Some Handel portraits considered' (Smith) 52
Some say, compar'd (Tweedledum and Tweedledee) 21
Sommer, O 72
Songs, Handel's A Lewis on 51
Sosarme performed in London 25
South Sea Bubble 21
Spectator, The 16
Spengel, J 72
Spiegl, F 89
Spohr, L 35
Squire, W B 87, 88; *The Handel manuscripts* in the King's Music Library 58
Staak, P van der 76
Stanley, J 39
Stanmore, Little 19
Steele, Sir R 16
Steffani, A 13, 17
Stefans, H *see* Rackwitz, W and Stefans, H
Steglich, R 65, 66, 69, 71, 84, 87
Stein, F 74, 78, 84
Stein, J 74
Stern, J 72
Stevens, D 76
Stone, D 83
Stone, N 72
Story of Handel's Messiah (Shaw)
Stradella, A 29
Straube, K 74, 79
Streatfeild, R A *Handel* 49; *Handel autographs in the British Museum* 58; *Handel, Canons and the Duke of Chandos* 49

Stuart, Prince C E 37
Style, Handel's, G Abraham on 51
Suites de pièces pour le clavecin 20, 51
Susanna performed in London 37
Sweeney, O *see* Macswiney

Tamerlano performed in London 23
Tarr, E H 82
Tasso's *Gerusalemme liberata* 14
Tate, P 83
Taust, D Handel's mother *see* Handel, D née Taust
Taylor, S 48, 78 *The indebtedness of Handel to other composers* 48
Taylor, S de B 75
Te deum, Dettingen 36; Utrecht, 15, 17, 26
Telemann, G P 9, 10, 30, 42; *Musique de table* of 30
Terpsicore, performed in London 27
Tertis, L 86
Teseo performed in London 15
Textual and historical companion to Handel's Messiah (Shaw) 54
Theodora performed in London 38-40
Theseus see *Teseo*
This is the day (Wedding anthem) 26
Tippett, Sir M 75
Tobin, J 65, 72; *Handel at work* 53-55; *Handel's Messiah, a critical account* 55
Tolomeo performed in London 24
Townsend, H *Account of the visit of Handel to Dublin* 52
Trionfo del tempo . . . performed in Rome 12, 13; in London 28
Triumph of time and truth (English version of above) 75
Troutbeck, J 77
Tustin, W 86
Tweedledum and Tweedledee see *Some say, compar'd*
Tyers, 41

Upmeyer, W 86
Urio, F A 48

Vauxhall Gardens 38, 41, 52
Venice, Handel in 12

Veröffentlichungen der Händel-Gesellschaft 61
Vespasiano (Ariosti) 23
Victoria and Albert Museum, London, Handel's statue in 52
Vollbach, F 73
Voluntary or a flight of angels and other pieces for Clay's musical clock 88
Walcha, M 81
Walker, A D 79
Walker, F G 72
Walpole, Sir R 24
Walsh, J 14, 59
Waltz, G W C Smith on 52
Water music, date and first performance etc of the 17, 18, 20; missing autograph of 54; W C Smith on 52
Wasner, F 75
Ways of Zion do mourn (Funeral anthem) 28
Wedding anthem for Princess Anne (*This is the day*) 26
Weinstock, H (*Handel*) 50
Weissmann, W 74, 80, 82
Wenzel, E 66, 78
Wenzinger, A 70
Were, Mrs 18

Wesley, C 80
Wesley, S 80
West, J E 72
Westrup, Sir J 56
Whitchurch, St Lawrence's church at 19, 49
Whittaker, W G 69
Williams, C F A *Handel, his life and works* 48, 50
Williams, P 70, 71
Willner, A 80
Woehl, W 86
Wolff, E 69, 71
Woodgate, L 79
Wright, D 83
Wunderer, A 80

Xerxes see *Serse*

Young, P 65, 74, 83; *Handel* 50; 'Handel the man' 51; *The oratorios of Handel* 53

Zachau or Zachow, F W 7, 9
Zadok the priest performed in London 24
Zanoskar 87
Zenck, H 75
Zingel, H J 88
Zschoch, F 66, 69, 70